THE SKY ISLAN
OF SOUTHEAST ARIZONA

Kate Crowley and Mike Link

Additional photography by
David Collister   Ed Cooper   Dick Dietrich
Ralph Fisher, Jr.   Greg Gnesios   Mary Jean Hage   Jim Honcoop
George Huey   David Lazaroff   Hiram Parent   Laurence Parent
Lynn Rogers   Noel and Helen Snyder   Lynn Stone

VOYAGEUR PRESS

To Little Shea
May lots of sun shine
in your life

Printed in Singapore

89 90 91 92 93   5 4 3 2 1

Library of Congress Cataloging-in-Publication Data

Crowley, Kate.
  The Sky Islands of southeast Arizona / Kate Crowley and Mike Link.
     p.   cm.
  ISBN 0-89658-105-5 : $14.95
     1. Natural history — Arizona. 2. Arizona — Description and travel.
  I. Link, Michael. II. Title.
  QH105.A65C76 1989   89-16419
  508.791 — dc20   CIP

Published by Voyageur Press, Inc.
P.O. Box 338
123 North Second Street
Stillwater, MN 55082 U.S.A.
In Minn 612-430-2210
Toll Free 800-888-9653

Voyageur Press books are also available at discounts in bulk quantities for premium or sales-promotion use. For details contact the Marketing Manager.

Please write or call for our free catalog of natural history publications.

CONTENTS

A NATURALIST'S VIEW

BY MIKE LINK

There is always a moment of hesitation when I tell someone I am going to southeastern Arizona. "You mean the Southwest, don't you?" is a typical response, but *the Southwest* is generic: it's a combination of states, physical and metaphysical. Southeast Arizona is like no other place. It is a collection of high mountains surrounded by desert seas, of spruce and pine forests perched on peaks that overlook the saguaro cactus of the Sonoran desert and the creosote bush of the Chihuahuan desert.

These are islands of rock, islands of vegetation, and islands of wildlife, where two desert seas come together, like the Atlantic and Pacific at the Cape. Desert life overlaps, mountain life is isolated. The desert plains and bajadas reach temperatures that will fry eggs on solar-heated rocks, while the mountain peaks collect snow and freezing temperatures.

The "Sky Islands" were once ocean islands, but that was too long ago for human memory; that was in a time that can be reconstructed only in the wit and imagination of geologists and wizards. The rock that is exposed is twisted and varied; it hoards precious metals, and reflects deep earth tones in the low-angle rays of sunrises and sunsets.

There are lava rocks, schists, granites, and gneisses, which are layered, jointed, eroded, and folded. The complexity of the rocks reaches its zenith in the Tucson Mountains, where the name of the formation is the Tucson Mountain Chaos. Geologists look at the taffy pull of hot-rock layers and shake their heads. Uplift here was not just a single event; these southeastern mountains were part of the Laramide, mid-tertiary, and basin-and-range mountain buildings. Where seas and lakes once stood, today there are playas.

Cold air may sink from the heads of Dos Cabezas and become a swirling dust devil in the Willcox Playa. The dust does a dervish dance across the flats toward the ghostly towns of Pearce and Cochise, where today's inhabitants share their hometown with echoes of wilder pasts.

There are open-pit mines, cities that stake their fame on gunfights and gamblers, and ranches that require fifty acres per head of livestock. History buffs time-travel to this land for its memories, and naturalists flock for flocks of birds.

The great ecologist Merriam discovered that in America, gaining elevation is equivalent to traveling north. Here the north- and south-facing slopes are drastically different, the riparian zones are endangered and essential, and the wildlife and plant life are often endemic.

"Endemic" may be the vegetative equivalent of "incestuous"; isolation limits genetic options. Plants, which cannot move to mate, cross-pollinate over the centuries in much the same way that geneticists create new variations of crops. The mutations manifest themselves in new species that are limited to single ranges and valleys.

Animals, which are more mobile, follow the development of plant communities. Mexican species move northward to meet the southern edge of other species' ranges. Trogons, becards, and parrots don't exist naturally in other parts of the United States, but they mingle here with the red-breasted nuthatches and mountain chickadees. Butterflies are movable patches of color, but insect collectors aren't limited to the colorful. Black lights and light sheets glow in the summer nights while entomologists look for new species of nondescript moths or colorful new beetles.

This is a paradise for birder, botanist, and lepidopterist—banding nets for birds, hummingbird feeders, feeding stations for javelinas, marked lizards, radio-tagged mammals and birds, and scientists sorting through an overload of stimuli.

People come here to see and learn, for warmth, walking, horseback riding, camping, exploring. They find ghost towns, old missions, and Spanish ruins; missiles and military; Indians, buffalo soldiers, cowboys, gunfighters, and entrepreneurs; botanical and

The rocks tell part of the story of this diverse land. They hold clues for both the geologist and archaeologist. (G. Huey)

5

zoological parks that combine education and fascination.

They also find pollution in the Tucson basin, daily jet contrails, illegal border crossings, and legal migrations. The hot boredom of the freeway is suddenly broken by Texas Canyon, a silver mine belongs to a new generation of dreamers, and cattle graze in vegetation that looks highly unpalatable.

This is diversity, this is contrast, this is the attraction for the naturalist, historian, and adventurous traveler. This is the southeastern corner of the great Southwest.

We come for natural history and we get caught up in human history. We look for birds, plants, and mammals and find ourselves fascinated by people. We search out wild animal species and find our own, the most eccentric. Our tales of discovery are feathered, photosynthetic, and human.

We come here to be surprised, we come here to be lost and to find. We want to see things that crawl and wriggle. Our minds are excited by this land of mental gymnastics and our book is a reflection of our thoughts and the inspiration of the land and the people. Don't expect a travelogue; just share our fascination.

In a sea of sand and shrubs, a desert tortoise savors the succulent fruit of a prickly pear cactus. (G. Huey)

6

TUCSON MOUNTAIN MOSAIC

SAGUARO NATIONAL MONUMENT—Mike Link

Cactus grow in homes all across the continent. They are not restricted by geography when indoor conditions can be modified. But plants in people's homes don't reproduce, they don't fill the food larders of wildlife, nor do they provide homes for animals. Only the prickly pear, which grows as far north as the Peace River in Canada, and a species of mammalary cactus grow naturally in the northern United States.

In *The Cacti of Arizona*, Lyman Benson states, "Cacti may be recognized by the large, fleshy, usually leafless stems and by spines always (at least in juvenile stages) developed in areole (restricted places) on the stems." It is the one category of plants that most people feel comfortable identifying. In other parts of the world, euphorbia, although not part of the cactus family, has evolved to look like our cactus; but in the United States, if it grows wild and looks like a cactus, it probably is. There are 147 species in the United States, and 68 of these occur in Arizona.

Cactus leaves have been eliminated (with minor exceptions), and the trunks of the woody plants have become fleshy and photosynthetic. The stems have large storage cells for water and waxy surfaces to prevent water loss. The roots spread out in an underground net to catch water from the sparse desert rain. Some needles tip downward so that rain will be quickly directed by the "driptips" to areas where the roots can collect it. The ribs, joints, and curvature of the stems also promote water flow. Any water trapped on the surface of the plant would quickly evaporate and be lost.

The saguaro is a symbol of the Sonoran desert. It is the classic cactus of comic strips, pop art, and postcard. An old rotting saguaro sheds its pleats and flesh and becomes a woody carcass that resembles the sacred Kachina dolls of the Hopi Indians. The living tree supports nesting birds and rodents in its cavities. It provides food for birds, mammals, insects, and people

when the creamy white flower is replaced by a luscious sweet red fruit that is full of seeds. I have tasted them and know why they are highly prized.

A saguaro grows an average of one-half inch per year, depending on water, temperature, the placement of a host such as palo verde, and the direction of the slope. It begins in the shade of a "nurse" plant and takes nine to ten years to reach six inches. After 25 years it is only three to four feet tall. Arms (branches) don't form until the cactus is over ten feet (75 years). It takes 150 years to reach thirty-five feet, and the plant may live to be 200, reaching a height of nearly forty feet.

The saguaro clings to desert soil by thin roots, and it sways easily in the wind. The arms are balancers, growing out to counterbalance the lean of the cactus. The thin roots extend great distances in a circle around the cactus, with a radius equal to the height of the plant; and the taproot is little more than three feet long.

In its lifetime, the mature cactus will produce twelve million seeds, but only one percent will even begin growing. They are finicky in youth, requiring a temperature of no more than seventy-seven degrees to germinate—that is why they need the shade of a "nurse." In addition, desert foragers, desperate for any good source of nutrition, will eat up any seed they find.

Sometimes the cactus will grow to a fan-shaped apex. About one in 200,000 has this growth disorder, where arms do not form properly. These not only are unusual to look at but are targets for collectors. In 1986, a couple from Arizona stole "Old Grandad," a 150-year-old treasure on Bureau of Land Management land. Because another couple from Oregon reported it missing, Fish and Wildlife officers were able to trace it to Yuma, and then to Las Vegas, where it was repossessed and returned to the Phoenix Desert Botanical Gardens.

This was just one case of cactus rustling among

Saguaro cactus in bloom. (G. Huey)

9

thousands that take place. Only the very distinctive shape of Old Grandad made it possible to prove its theft.

Saguaro National Monument, with units on both the east and west sides of Tucson, is a reservoir of cactus growth and reproduction, as well as protection. The national monument is more than a plant garden; it preserves a national treasure. Located in both the Rincon and the Tucson mountains, it looks down on one of the world's fastest-growing metropolitan areas. Buildings displace saguaro at the mountain's feet, smog drifts up the valleys to upset delicate respiration, and wildlife becomes condensed and less mobile.

In the Rincon and the Tucson mountains you can feel the conflicting tensions of plant communities. The taller Rincon Mountains have over seventy species of birds, fifteen mammals, and six hundred plants that are not in the hotter, shorter Tucson range. The eastern half receives more rain and snow.

I came to the "desert" years ago, with visions of the Foreign Legion in my brain. I pictured saguaros and sand dunes. I expected a camel desert of Arabs and oases in a garden of Sonoran desert plants. But that was not what I found. This was not sandy soil, it was rocky debris, a *bajada* (a skirt around old mountains)—the litter that has washed down and slowly moved toward the playas at the bottom of the valley. This was a land of fractured highlands and rubble soil, with fifteen to twenty thousand saguaros per square mile.

In the midst of the saguaro were different layers of shrubs, like miniature forests, and other armored members of the cactus family.

Besides the large saguaro, there are barrel cactus with fishhook spines and squatty, thick stems; prickly pear, which range further than any other cactus, grow faster, and stabilize loose soil; hedgehog cactus, which have long porcupinelike spines, multiple stems in a cluster, and flowers that range from red to blue and all the shades of violet. Hedgehog flowers may measure three inches, while the stem is less than ten.

Cholla (pronounced *choya*) cactus is the prickliest cactus group. The teddy bear cholla is the most easily recognized. Its numerous yellow spines look disarmingly soft from a distance, but the joints are brittle, causing them to break off and hitchhike on passersby. Because the spines stick to shoes, shirt, and skin, it seems as though the plant is throwing itself at the passing person, and one species has been nicknamed "jumping cholla."

Buckhorn cholla is less spiny and looks like antlers from a distance. Pencil cholla is thin, with red fleshy fruit at the stem tips. Desert Christmas cactus has red fruits and very long spines. Some chollas are full grown at less than a foot tall, while the chain fruit cholla is treelike and twelve feet tall, with a four-inch trunk. Mammalaria cactus are breast-shaped (if you have been in the desert sun for too many hours or have a good imagination). Botanists describe the various

forms as cylindroid, globose, or turbinate. They are short plants, usually rounded on top, with two sizes of spines. The spines are dense and give a soft texture to the plant.

I have tasted not only the wonderful fruit of the saguaro but also the nut of the jojoba. This plant has become the wonder plant of the desert. Its unusual liquid wax is now gathered in commercial jojoba fields for shampoos, lotions, and lubricants that are very stable in high-heat conditions. This oil is reducing the collection of whale oil, and in the long run may do more to save the whale than the ineffective world treaties that we struggle with. In addition, the nut has the taste of a roasted almond.

The jojoba is wind pollinated and utilizes two upright leaves to deflect air currents and bring the pollen home to the female flower. Once the seeds are produced, another desert story begins, because they require an absence of light, a high soil moisture, and a very narrow range of temperatures to germinate. Those conditions are found in the burrow of Bailey's pocket mouse. This mouse gathers as many as two pounds of jojoba seeds for storage in its subterranean home and gradually consumes the nuts. The few that are not eaten germinate and propagate.

What makes this story even more remarkable is the fact that the seeds have a toxicity that affects most rodents, but the Bailey's mouse has evolved a method of detoxifying the nut.

Another good taste is the seeds of the palo verde—a pea-bean flavor. These seeds were gathered by Indians and Mexicans for food. The shrub, the main shade source on the desert, has tiny leaves and carries chlorophyl in its thin bark.

The monument is also home to desert wildlife. Gila woodpeckers and gilded flickers open the large cactus stems and create homes for owls. Costa's hummingbirds feed at the flowers. Gambel's quail grunt, cackle, chuckle, and make plaintive calls, or a more gregarious four-note call. They blend with the vegetation, then scurry down the arroyos and trails with their topknots waving.

Roadrunners dash across the pavement and through the campgrounds chasing lizards; curve-billed thrashers and cactus wrens call from saguaro tops and make nice silhouettes in the rising sun. The cactus wren is a gregarious bird and sings at dawn and all through the day. Its song is fifteen to thirty notes long and is startling more than musical.

The cactus wren makes a nest that is bulky and well-armed by the protective spines of the cholla cactus. The nests also have other special attributes, which are different from most birds'. For one thing, adults and young stay in different nests, which are close to one another. The nests are also designed for cooling efficiency. The young defecate onto the nest floor, which adds moisture to the cavity, and the nest hole faces the prevailing wind, which increases airflow and evaporation.

The mammals in the monument include spotted and

(E. Cooper)

Fishhook cactus. (G. Huey)

11

striped skunks, kit fox, coyote, black-tailed jackrabbit, desert cottontail, and mule deer. The coyote is conspicuous since it frequently sings to the campers, and the rabbits are seen along the trail because they move around in the daylight.

The monument has trails to hike, floral displays in the springtime, birds to observe, and a combination of geologic and biologic wonders.

Saguaro National Monument, like all refuges, is too small and too vulnerable. It needs concern, care, and ecological management in the surrounding land, as well as within its borders. A park is more than a monument to nature's diversity, it is a deposit in our cultural savings account, which might make the difference for our survival into the future. Plants are disappearing rapidly from the world as humans manipulate and destroy; but plants like the jojoba still exist in the wild, beneficial plants for the plate and the pharmacy, still awaiting discovery. We cannot be complacent — we are still dependent on nature, and we always will be.

ARIZONA SONORA DESERT MUSEUM — Kate Crowley

I sat on a bench at the Arizona Sonora Desert Museum on a bright January morning, letting the sun warm me, when out of the corner of my eye, I caught sight of a cactus wren moving rapidly among the rock and leaf litter. It would walk a few steps, then bend down and lift a stone with its bill. It continued on a zigzag path, searching, but coming up empty beaked, until it was only two feet away from me. There it stopped next to a small, round mammillaria cactus and began to pick at the cottony white material that was packed between the plant's ridges. It made quick repeated stabs until its bill was filled with the downy fibers.

Then it turned and made a short, upward-swooping flight, across the path to a soap tree yucca. It disappeared momentarily among the long green and brown fronds, but soon flew back out and began its collection process once again.

It amazed me that the bird was able to make such rapid, well-aimed stabs into a space no more than one-quarter inch wide, and protected on all sides by whorls of sharp spines. For that matter, how is the cactus wren able to stand on top of a cactus, as I saw one do, and not suffer from the upright thorns?

The bird has an absolute affinity for things sharp and thorny. It often builds its globular nest in dense cholla cactus, a cactus whose spines are capable of piercing shoe leather, yet the wren hops around the plant without noticeable difficulty. Since its ability to do so has never been satisfactorily explained, I propose that it has developed a mystical ability, similar to walking on fire or lying on a bed of nails.

As I sat on the bench, surrounded by numerous cactus and desert shrubs, as well as the birds that use them for food and shelter, the only reminders of where I actually was were the sounds of excited schoolchildren, scuffling along, laughing and squealing with the adventure of a field trip, and the loud squawking of thick-billed parrots in their circular enclosures.

The Arizona Sonora Desert Museum, which opened in 1952, is designed to show us just how complex and important are the interrelationships of land, water, plants, wildlife, and people of the Sonoran desert region.

Founder William Carr was a former associate curator at the American Museum of Natural History who came to the Sonoran desert under doctor's orders. He was a scientist and a humanist, who saw the great diversity that existed in this dry and misunderstood land. He wrote that he wanted others to share in his discoveries, "as a means of helping man to recognize and assume his responsibilities toward nature in order to gain some hope of assuring his future."

The museum buildings are neutral in color and keep a low profile, barely rising above the nearby saguaros, so it is easy to forget that you're in a botanical zoo. Many of the exhibits are based on natural habitat design, using artificial rockwork and living plants to imitate the animals' natural homes. Most importantly, the animals are representative of the Sonoran desert. Encompassing only fifteen acres, the museum is located within Tucson Mountains County Park and borders the Saguaro National Monument (western unit), so the sense of spaciousness is great.

The cactus and succulent garden, described as a comprehensive regional collection, is a very good place to observe the adaptations of living things for survival in a desert environment. The palo verde tree has green bark, which allows photosynthesis to occur even when the tree is leafless. The shrubby creosote bush, the most prevalent plant in the Chihuahuan desert, drops its leaves to reduce water loss during dry seasons, but leafs out as soon as the rains return. The ocotillo looks like a cluster of thorny sticks during dry periods, but within forty-eight hours of a rain, it is covered with soft, tender leaves, which last as long as the moisture.

Succulents evolved and adapted to the desert by storing water within their tissues. Having become water reservoirs, those with a means of protection from thirsty animals and the drying sun survived to reproduce. Many succulents have spines that dissipate heat and prevent grazing, while others use toxicity (poison) as protection. Succulents may also have waxy coatings on their skins, which prevents water loss; few, if any, small leaves; and ribs or pleats, which allow the plant to expand when water is available.

All plants must respire, in order to live — but through respiration, moisture is lost. In order to minimize this, succulents evolved a special variation of photosynthesis called CAM (crassulacean acid metabolism). Through this process the plant's stomates (pores in leaves or stems) open at night, rather than in the day, to take in carbon dioxide and release oxygen. In the cooler, more humid air of nighttime, only a small amount of moisture is lost.

After my visit to the cactus and succulent garden, I

The gila woodpecker excavates nest holes in saguaro cactus. (J. Honcoop)

Two young roadrunners peer out from under their mother as she sits on her well-camouflaged nest. (D. Lazaroff)

entered the building that holds the insects and reptiles. No two groups of creatures elicit more fascination and revulsion in people. All around me I could hear people struggling with their fears and mixed emotions.

"You're not going to get me to go in there, there's snakes in there!"

"Wow! Look at that one there."

"Is that a gila monster? I want to see that, but I don't want to walk past that snake."

"Oh my god! I can't even look at it."

"Venomous. That means poisonous."

Standing near the insect displays I heard conflicting opinions.

"Oooh—ugly!"

"Oh how neat."

With time, the people begin to look closer and relax a bit. They read the descriptions of the animals above the displays and discuss with one another what they've learned.

"Boy, now doesn't that one fit in the desert."

I watched a three-inch-long tarantula hawk feeding on a large red grape. It had black legs, thorax, and head, but its wings were a rich, velvety russet. This is a nectar-feeding wasp, but the female becomes a predator when she is ready to lay her eggs. This requires a tarantula, a spider that greatly outweighs the wasp. The "hawk" stings the spider, paralyzing it, and then drags the huge body into an underground nest. It lays an egg on the spider's body, and the hatchling emerges to find itself sitting on top of its food supply.

Looking in another display, I found a desert stink beetle, also called a pinacate. I had seen these shiny black-shelled beetles along the trail at the Patagonia Sanctuary. They have an interesting habit of bending forward when disturbed, lifting their abdomens high in the air. What I hadn't noticed was the foul-smelling substance that they release while posturing.

This odor is intended to discourage predators, but the grasshopper mouse has found a way to avoid the defense. The mouse grabs the beetle and thrusts its rear end into the ground, then consumes the beetle from the head down.

Like a game of poker, nature is a process of bluff and raise. The process of adaptation is never finished. The environment constantly changes and so must the inhabitants.

In the reptile room there was a docent, who calmly and clearly answered the questions and corrected the misinformation that the visitors posed. "Venom is used primarily for food-getting, and it starts the digestive process. The snake strikes, releases its venom, then releases the animal, which dies."

Another docent in the next room held a docile tarantula on her open palm for visitors to inspect. Understandably there was surprise and awe in many visitors' reactions.

A large graphic compares the venomous Arizona coral snake with seven other species that closely resemble it but are nonvenomous. It is a good graphic, intended to teach people not to jump to conclusions,

—what you think is dangerous may in fact be quite harmless. But the similarities are so close that reaction to any snake, especially in a highly emotional situation, would likely be negative. The man beside me said, "Boy that's confusing. Who can figure all that out when the snake is curling around your ankle?"

The Desert Museum goal is to teach people to better understand their environment, to help them appreciate the concept of adaptation. It is a concept that is just as applicable to the human species as it is to any of the plants or animals that live in the Sonoran desert. In fact, it is critical for people to understand the meaning of adaptation to their surroundings, because unlike the animals and plants, we believe we are capable of surviving outside of nature's rules. Founder Bill Carr expressed the sense of urgency that faces us when he said, "The time for widespread implementation of this kind of endeavor [the Museum] is now, before man succeeds in totally defiling his habitat and making it unlivable."

LAZY K BAR RANCH—Kate Crowley

There is another endangered species in the desert surrounding the spreading metropolis of Tucson—the dude ranch. Some will say, "So what? Who needs them anyway?" but dude ranches let their guests explore both nature and history.

Horses have been a part of the Arizona landscape for the past four hundred years, ever since the first Spanish explorers arrived. They were assimilated into the Indian culture and were integral to the white pioneers' ensuing exploration and settlement. Until the last half of this century, when the Southwest became the mecca for sun seekers and retirees, the horse played a vital role in the economy of the area.

The first dude ranches developed around 1900 as a response to a desire by eastern city slickers, or "dudes," to live out the romantic fantasy of the Wild West. With each passing decade, rural populations have declined and new urban generations have grown up with a fascination for the mystique of the cowboys and the land and animals they tried to tame.

Growing up in the city, I dreamed of owning a horse and riding free, like the wind, through brush and grassland. My frequent begging to go "horseback riding" got me out to a local stable with some regularity, but a horse of my own did not materialize until I was thirty-seven years old, and a visit to a real dude ranch didn't happen until I was thirty-eight. We may repress our childhood dreams, but they never really go away.

The Lazy K Bar Ranch sits amid a rocky desert scrub community, just north of Tucson and above the floodplain of the Santa Cruz River. It was over one hundred degrees at noon when we drove past freshly laid-out curbs and symmetrical plots, through the white gates, and up the dirt road to the office. Saguaro cactus stood like sentries along the drive, and deep purple-brown rocks rose ahead of us.

Carol Moore, the manager, arrived at the ranch in

The tarantula is a large and formidable looking spider, but its bite is no worse than a bee sting. (G. Huey)

The thorns of the cholla cactus are capable of piercing leather, yet the cactus wren safely builds its nest among the cactus's branches. (L. Stone)

1975 and has been there ever since, except for a four-year hiatus. She has lived all over the United States but felt a strong pull to this arid land. Like so many others, she has been influenced by the authors of the Western genre, in her case so much so that she named her son Zane.

We were in time to catch the end of the flowering season for the saguaro. The big white blossoms open during late April, May, and June, but the lifespan of an individual flower is short; it opens a few hours after sunset one day and wilts by the next afternoon. The sequence continues night after night, until as many as one hundred flowers have blossomed on a single saguaro. In their brief existence, the blooms attract a variety of birds, bats, and insects that feed on the nectar and spread pollen from blossom to blossom.

In June and July the saguaro fruit ripens into the sweet, juicy pulp and dark, glistening seeds that attract numerous birds even in the heat of midday. Steve, the head wrangler, told us later that to him, "It's like they flower twice, once with the real flower and then again when the fruits ripen and pop open into four petal shapes, a deep red color."

As we watched from our covered veranda, little Gambel's quail, with their curlycue topknots, garbled as they wandered from one shrub to the next. Gila woodpeckers flew to holes in the tall, many-armed saguaros and disappeared inside to their well-protected nests.

Doves — white-winged, Inca, and ground — cooed and fluttered from shrub to shrub. We listened to a cactus wren loudly scold as it perched on the mane of a ceramic burro. Nearby, tucked protectively in the prickly branches of a cholla cactus, was its nest.

High in the top of a towering cabbage palm tree, a hooded oriole had made its nest. We watched as a Cassin's kingbird with custard-colored breast darted up from a palm frond to snatch an insect out of the air and settle back down on the tree. All of the plants and wildlife combined with the turquoise pool to give the compound the atmosphere of an oasis.

We asked Carol Moore about the wildlife, and she said, "There are bobcats in the area, and lots of coyotes and a few deer. I've seen fewer snakes in the last few years, but more roadrunners [known snake predators]." She also talked about the javelinas: "They really get people's blood going. They'll get right up on the porch. We had some people from Sweden here one time, and when they went to their room, there were wild pigs blocking their way. The came rushing back, trying to explain what was wrong, but they couldn't speak English very good, so we had a heck of a time trying to figure it out."

We had our own encounter with the wild pigs one night during our stay at the Lazy K Bar. My daughter Alyssa had gone on ahead, and before we left the main building, she came in breathless, to say there was a family of javelinas in front of our rooms. Mike and my son Jon hurried back, while I finished putting away a film.

Because of my delay, I missed seeing the family of seven, milling and rooting around at the base of the saguaros. There were a few babies in the group, and Alyssa said, "You should have seen them, Mom, they were so cute and about the size and shape of small watermelons." They had run around behind our building, where we could hear them munching away in the darkness.

We scouted around the brush, where we could hear a couple of them snorting and snarling. They are shy of people, but fights sometimes break out in a group. They have short, straight tusks that fit so closely together that they hone one another to razor sharpness with each snap of the jaws. This gives them a similarity to spear-edged javelins, hence the common name, javelinas. They are also known as collared peccaries because of a lighter-colored band of hair just behind the neck. Overall, their coat is a dark, grizzled gray.

In our flashlight beam they looked like big gray mice from the side, but from the front they looked like very skinny, hairy pigs. Javelinas are about two feet high and three feet long, and an average adult weighs forty to fifty pounds. Although they resemble pigs, they are not related. The two families diverged forty to seventy million years ago.

They travel in groups of mixed ages and sexes, foraging as they go. Their food consists mainly of vegetable matter, but they have complex stomachs to aid in the digestion of coarsely chewed food. Their diet includes prickly pear cactus, spines and all.

We saw fewer animals during our early morning trail rides, but that was not surprising; by 8:00 A.M., the temperatures were in the nineties. Our wrangler took us on a trail that led past a couple of little brown long-legged burrowing owls. One was on top of a saguaro, but it flew down to the ground to stand by its partner and the nest hole as we rode past. They made chattering sounds at us, but did not flee.

The trails wind through a flat land of mesquite and creosote bush, the latter covered with fuzzy little balls of seed. The ground is a combination of loose rock and sand, and I was amazed at the horses' ability to keep their footing in such shifting terrain, especially when we began to climb into the nearby hills.

The path is so narrow it does not allow two people to walk side by side, but the horses have followed it numerous times. The human tendency, of course, is to pull back on the reins to slow your descent, but that only pulls the horse's head up and away from its visual pathfinding. If you give it enough rein so that it can look down at the trail, the horse carefully picks its way through and around the chunks of rock. Even with a loose rein, the horse's back feet may slip a little, and you grip the saddle horn a little tighter, but the horse just keeps plodding along, up and over the crest of the hill and back down the other side.

Behind us was the flat Santa Cruz River valley. It is a river floodplain and was once rich in soil and grass, a historic and bountiful expressway for the herds of cattle that were driven to market. But their constant

A family of javelinas makes a meal of a prickly pear cactus—spines and all. (L. Rogers)

movement and grazing destroyed the topsoil, while erosion soon shipped the nutrients downriver. No grass grows there anymore, just a river of asphalt on the freeway and houses that sprout and spread over the terrain.

In front of us grew saguaro, including the oldest one on the 160 acres. It was a gnarled old plant in the last throes of life. Its skin was shrinking, and at the base, woody ribs were exposed. Grazing compacts the ground around the cactus, which not only kills seedlings but can slowly kill the nurse tree as well. Severe droughts or hard frosts can also kill them, and this part of Arizona is at the extreme northern and eastern edge of the saguaro range. Here they are occasionally exposed to very cold winter temperatures.

But even as they die, they can give life. As we rode around the elderly cactus, we could hear the faint chirping of birds, coming from one of the holes in an outstretched arm.

Carol Moore was not overly optimistic about the future of the Lazy K Bar Ranch. She says, "Most people come because of the horses." But with only 160 acres and more and more people building homes nearby, there will soon be little room for trail rides. When people buy two- or three-acre plots, they like to build fences and they don't like caravans of horseback riders parading through their front yards.

Carol remembers the times, not so long ago, when they could sit on the patio, look out and see nothing of civilization. Now, the air has become hazy with desert dust that is stirred up as the bulldozers work.

She is skeptical about civilization's ability to tame the river that flows through the future development. "In 1983, the Santa Cruz River flooded and we could look out and see white caps. Now a thirty-million dollar development is going in. Supposedly, they have flood control on the river now."

There will always be those who only see the need for "growth and development," but there are others who feel different and wish they could alter the course we're taking. Carol expresses that view: "To those of us who live here, who have Tucson in our heart, it's gut wrenching."

17

THE SANTA CATALINA MOUNTAINS

BY MIKE LINK

Tucson's back wall is 9,157 feet high and includes a ski slope. This is the Santa Catalina mountain range, with Mount Lemmon at its summit, a range offering diversity and easy access. The steady stream of cars up and down the mountain testifies to its beauty and people's interest. In the winter, skiers, tubers, and sledders journey to the heights, and hikers stay in the lowlands. In the summer, picnickers go to the coolness of the high country and the shade of northern conifers, while birdwatchers look for everything from nuthatches and olive warblers to roadrunners and cactus wrens.

A drive up to the peak begins in saguaro and palo verde, on sparse slopes of weathered granite. There are vistas of Tucson and the distant Santa Ritas, as well as the Tucson and Rincon ranges. It is a skyscape of blue peaks repeated over and over into the horizon, shades of blue and violet separated by sharp outlines of rugged sculpted ranges.

The road twists back and forth across a steep ravine, but each switchback seems to enter a new and unseen landscape. The perspective of elevation is mixed with changes in plant communities and variation in rock weathering. In the cactus lands the rocks are cut by road construction, and they show distinct bands of gray and black. They are metamorphosed rocks, rocks that cooled beneath the surface and flowed into cracks, or melted the adjoining layers.

In sedimentary rocks, layers indicate water deposition, but in igneous rocks like these, they indicate remelting and sorting of minerals—cracking and filling, stretching and oozing, rearranging and changing. Minerals disappear in the heat and pressure, and new minerals grow in the same turbulent magma. Large crystals catch the sunlight and glow, dark bands absorb the heat, and all the layers tilt and dip from the energies of the earth's mountain-building forces.

Here where rock is visible and panoramic viewpoints let you sweep the horizon, the story of the land is hard to ignore. The formation of metamorphic rocks took place 1.6 billion years ago, beneath the sea.

Sediments were melted and transformed by the intrusion of mantle magmas. The seas continued, and marine organisms flourished. Near present-day Bisbee, a reef formation developed in the Mesozoic.

Then fifty to eighty million years ago, the Santa Catalinas and the Santa Ritas formed as part of a large mountain complex that preceded the Rockies. The mountains rose and stood tall during the formation of the Tucson range and the Chiricahuas. The Catalinas were docile mountains compared to the violent neighbors of the tertiary. The younger ranges formed by volcanism, violent eruptions that lit the sky, both day and night.

The birth of so many mountains, the separation of the continents, the growth of the Rockies, and the combination of forces tore at the landscape, creating giant faults. The earth rose and collapsed in basins and ranges, while it buckled and folded in the Rockies.

The road sweeps up a brushy canyon and into the oak/grass/sotol complex. Here the rocks are weathering into boulders, layers are separating out and being rounded by wind and water. They roll down the creeks or slopes, or sit like partially buried heads among the shrubs. Weathering has gone on for all the millions of years that the rock has existed. The forces of nature are always breaking down what they build, recycling, and changing the earth. A mountain is not permanent; it only seems so to humans, with our short life spans.

The rock is made of many minerals, and some are weaker than others. Erosion attacks the weaknesses, dissolving, eliminating the weak and separating the strong. The loss of the soft minerals in the mix loosens and fragments the rock. Pieces fall off, and they are transported by gravity. They may split by impact, be dissected by probing roots, or be weakened further by the acids of decaying plant matter. The large pieces of the bajada are slowly reduced to mineral grains, to the stronger quartz grains, which will roll down in rain and runoff until they accumulate in the washes as

Sabino Canyon. (D. Lazaroff)

Mule deer. (J. Honcoop)

The coyote is a highly adaptable animal that has learned to survive and prosper in harsh environments. (G. Huey)

sand.

The granite becomes tall and columnar. Here deep joints form parallel planes and erosion has broadened the natural cracks. Vertical cracks, horizontal layers, tilted strata. It is abstract art at its best. People look at the hoodoos (the isolated columns) and give them names, but the names represent one person's perspective. They are better ignored. Art is beyond naming; it is a visual experience that triggers emotions and responses in the observer. Look for your own impression, see light and shadow, colors, depth, arrangement, hoodoo set against the wispy mare's tails of the sky or the solid deep-green cloak of the upper elevations.

Oaks become more prominent, and they are joined by manzanitas, junipers, and pines. Patches of snow appear as the pines become more and more dominant. The communities keep changing, not just because of elevation but also because of the direction and the steepness of the slope. Steepness may prevent a plant from taking root, or water from seeping into the soil, and the direction the slope faces may intensify the solar energy or block it altogether. The conifers grow lower on the north face, the cactus reach higher on the south.

Hikers, climbers, sightseers all cluster on the peaks. The town below may be their home, but this is the feast for souls, the place of recreation and renewal.

CATALINA STATE PARK

A coyote moved easily through the mesquite, loose-limbed and jaunty. It sauntered across the road and into the shrubs on the other side with hardly a glance back. Its tail streamed behind, large enough to look like something following the animal. A second coyote followed thirty yards behind the first, a little more wary, a little more attentive. It reached the road, stopped, and looked at the car, veered back into the shrubs, and took a slightly faster gait to move ahead onto the road and then dart across to join its buddy.

The coyote is highly adaptive, adjusting to all the changes that have accompanied human development. It was once thought to be the symbol of the West, its sad wail serving as the mantra of the desert and sagebrush country, but that is no longer true. The elimination of wolves over much of the United States has hastened the spread of the coyote throughout the continent.

As it is with all predators, the livestock lost to these animals is grossly exaggerated. The coyote consumes about two hundred pounds a year, which the Desert Museum says is equal to seventy-five jackrabbits, one hundred cottontails, or five thousand rodents. The coyote's service to humans is far greater than its harm. The effect of humans' war on coyotes has been to eliminate the weak and less adapted individuals, to destroy thousands of competitors, and to leave the coyote much stronger and faster than in the past. Like all programs of wanton killing, predator control is ineffective, and a waste of life and money.

We saw the coyotes in a sanctuary, a place where they and mule deer and javelinas can browse, where trails lead to the bighorn sheep and the white-tailed deer. This is Catalina State Park, a gateway to the Santa Catalina Mountains and the Pusch Ridge Wilderness.

Mesquite abounds where the land was once grazed by domestic stock, but native plants surround the wash and line the hillsides. We watched black-tailed jackrabbits bound and chase one another, their long ears tipped with black, their tails marked with a black spot.

Red-tailed hawks sat in the shrubs, small birds flitted among dense cover, and tracks in the sandy wash marked the movement of unseen animals.

The park is not itself spectacular; it is instead a buffer for the mountains, for the bighorn sheep that are threatened by the diseases of domestic sheep, from the impact of too much recreation in one area. We need a place to view the mountains from the north side—we need more parks like Catalina.

SABINO CANYON

It was January, but it felt like autumn to me as we walked along the gurgling stream, stepped from rock to rock, and zigzagged from shore to shore. The temperature was cool, and the trees still had color in their crowns. Ash trees held thick seed clusters, and cottonwood leaves were yellow. Beneath our feet we crunched the leaves of sycamore and willow. Kate felt like it was spring, with gilded woodpeckers squeaking in the shrubs, kinglets darting in the branches, and the sound of running water bubbling beneath us. Both of us carry our Minnesota experiences with us as we explore new places.

We are all products of our childhoods, we still see and feel the world in ways that are individual and related to the parks, homes, and people that shaped our youth. Even decades and thousands of miles can't change that perspective. That is why every visitor has his or her own memories, each person takes personal images and impressions along.

With that thought in mind, I found myself mentally drifting from the woody floodplain forests to the cactus slopes and into the schools of Tucson. Where we walked this afternoon, sixty kids had walked this morning, accompanied by volunteer naturalists. People who love the natural world have brought their energies from many places to reside in Tucson. Many are retired, but all are enthusiastic and full of dedication.

Thirty to forty people divide the responsibility of teaching Tucson youth about the natural history of the canyon. They work long hours, put up with some of kids' less admirable qualities, and get no money, but they are paid with the knowledge that the lessons of natural history and human responsibility will travel with the kids forever. These kinds of experiences and people are the real world savers.

The valley had more than an isolated tree or a line of bank dwellers. Here were actual groves. Titmice, Hutton's vireos, and nuthatches roamed the crowns of the trees, and a green-backed heron and a belted kingfisher scouted the stream for food. Fish live in these waters — organisms that lead totally aquatic lives can exist within one hundred feet of barrel cactus and saguaro.

We followed the stream to the dam, and then wandered into the mesquite flats along the park boundary. A small verdin was backlit by the lowering sun, and its golden head seemed to glow. A thrasher bounced around in the leaves beneath a creosote bush. Near the park entrance, a Gambel's quail darted in and out of the bushes, and a brazen roadrunner was the area beggar.

The canyon is protected by the National Forest Service, and the road, which was first used for pack animals, is closed to car traffic. A tram system replaces the automobile and protects the air quality and safety of the hiker. It is a land of natural beauty, but most important it is a monument to education and care.

Occasionally a winter storm slides down from the Santa Catalina Mountains and leaves a carpet of white on the desert plants. (D. Lazaroff)

The tiny elf owl is the most abundant owl in Arizona, yet only a few fortunate people will ever see one in the wild. (G. Huey)

THE RINCON MOUNTAINS

TANQUE VERDE RANCH—Kate Crowley

It was around 1:00 P.M. and we stood on the veranda of the main building, looking in disbelief at the thermometer hanging on a nearby support post. It registered 114 degrees Fahrenheit. No wonder there was so little activity going on around us.

Sitting sprawled on a bench behind us, next to the pink adobe walls, was an exhausted wrangler. He pulled out a big hankerchief, removed his hat, and mopped the sweat that covered his face and neck. Out in front of us came the periodic swish of a sprinkler, spraying water on a thirsty piece of lawn.

We had come to Tanque Verde Ranch in the middle of a record-breaking heat wave. The ranch has been around since the late 1800s, evolving over the years from a hardworking cattle ranch run by the Carrillo family to a semi-dude ranch when a Texas maverick ran it in the middle of this century. In the late 1950s, the Cote family purchased the ranch and developed it into the internationally known guest ranch/resort that it is today.

Only twelve miles east of Tucson, it sits surrounded on two sides by federal land. To the east is the Coronado National Forest and to the south is Saguaro National Monument. Standing on the porch in front of your room, you can look into the distance at a saguaro-studded desert of muted greens that gradually rises and changes to ridged foothills of brown and dusky purple. Some of the upper hills reach five thousand feet in height, more than three thousand feet higher than the ranch.

Although Tanque Verde easily qualifies as a luxury resort, it draws people as much for the opportunity to get on a horse and ride off into the sunset. We met one family that returns every year, just for that reason. They live in Milwaukee and never ride except when they come to Tanque Verde. Their family now includes three little girls, and as soon as they're able to hold onto the saddle horn and fit the shortest stirrups, they're up on the horses and going for daily rides. Their mother spends as many hours as possible on horseback.

This year she took advantage of a three-day pack trip up into the National Forest and one of those distant peaks. There was no luxury on that ride. They took no tents and the trails were steep and narrow, but it was the real thing for the city dweller who longed for adventure and a taste of an earlier lifestyle.

It rained for two days and nights on that ride, a horse got sick and had to be walked back, and the riders shivered through some cold, wet nights, but there were no complaints when they returned. They had tested their skills and their spirit, and lived on nature's terms.

Because of the extreme heat during the summer, there are only two rides a day, the first at 7:00 A.M. and the second at 10:00 A.M. At 7:00 A.M. the temperature was fairly comfortable—the sun actually felt good on the arms and neck. But an hour later, it had intensified enough to start beads of sweat rolling down the back.

The vegetation, although still a desert community, seemed more lush and abundant than we found in the Tucson Mountains. The trails were lined with tall, many-branched saguaros, prickly pear, and mesquite. We moved up and down through rocky washes, with the early morning light softening the bleached color of the gravel and sand. Sitting motionless under the cactus were a few desert cottontails, relying on their light brown fur and their frozen postures to hide them from our eyes.

I signed up for the loping ride with three other women and Dave, our guide/wrangler, who liked to ride fast and daring. He wore a black derby hat and was skinny enough to hide behind a saguaro. The other three women had been riding all week and sounded much more confident than I, so I kept my mount, Charro, a reddish roan, at the tail end of the line.

We walked out to an area that was flat and sandy, but still well covered with cactus and woody shrubs. Dave checked the cinches on our saddles once more before asking the group, "Do you want to do Dead Man's Curve fast or slow?" The other three readily

25

agreed on fast, and I just gripped the reins a little tighter. Dave raised his hand, and with a little yelp we were off.

This was not the straight, wide trail I'm used to riding back in the Midwest; this was a combination slalom/obstacle course. Charro was anxious to keep up with the other horses, but I was finding it difficult to keep up with him, since my stirrups were a little too long and my feet kept slipping out. I heard Dave yell, as he said he would, when we approached Dead Man's Curve, so I reined in a little more, and Charro and I managed to take the turn reasonably well. The next one was a little tougher because it was unexpected, and as Charro leaned to the left, centrifugal force pushed me right. Sheer willpower and a good grip on the pommel kept me in place.

Dave rechecked our saddles and I asked him to shorten my stirrups a bit. I told him the trouble I was having keeping my seat and he suggested, "Just sit back like you're in a rocking chair and keep your feet forward."

There was one last lope to do on this stretch and he described it as "a slalom course, with a few dips, but don't worry, they're not that deep, and then there's a hill to go up at the end."

My adrenaline was way up, along with my heartbeat, as he raised his fist for the takeoff. Trailing the other four horses meant that I was eating dust, but I could see well enough to know that a tumble off Charro would mean a painful landing on some thorny plant.

My stomach dropped with each dip, and I felt giddy with the thrill of riding like a real cowboy in wild country. My mind flashed back on memories of chase scenes on the Saturday morning TV shows, and I was riding with Roy Rogers, Hopalong Cassidy, the Cisco Kid, or Zorro.

Then we were swooping up the slope and coming to a halt, both horses and riders panting and all of us smiling and agreeing, "That was great."

The remainder of our ride took us up into the rocky hills, where we met the other morning riders for a breakfast cookout at the old homestead site. It was a large group of thirty or more, mostly made up of Italians who spoke little or no English. But appreciation of good food and magnificent scenery is a common language, and it was easy to interpret one Italian's "Que bella!" as he gazed out at the deep blue desert sky and the cactus covered hills.

* * *

Joe, a slight Mexican-American wrangler with a gray peppered beard, took Mike and me out for a sunset ride. He was a quiet, thoughtful man who had grown up right among these hills. Like more than one wrangler we had seen, he was limping—recovering from torn ligaments in his left ankle, acquired when a "green" horse had stumbled on the trail and fallen on him. You could see the pain on his face every time he

climbed into the saddle. I wondered how he was able to get tight-fitting cowboy boots on and off everyday.

Joe's grandparents homesteaded a section of land in the 1890s, at a time when there was still some danger of renegade Apache raids. His grandmother knew the medicinal uses of many of the desert plants, and Joe told us about using cottonwood leaves: "You boil them to make a poultice for sore muscles. It works. I've used it lots of times. They're sort of like eucalyptus leaves."

When Joe was growing up in Redington, he could look out the window of the schoolhouse and watch herds of cattle being driven past. But that seems like a long time ago now: "More and more hills are getting covered with houses."

Joe started working as a kid at a cattle ranch. Today, he chooses the riding stock for Tanque Verde. They'll buy twenty to thirty horses at a time, with thirty-day return policies on them. Joe says quarter horses have the best disposition. The horse I was riding was called Ghiribaldi. According to Joe, "He was a cattle ranch horse. They're the best kind. They've been well trained over and over and it's really well set in their minds. They're also used to a lot of action and distraction, so they're not easily spooked."

It was easy to see that Joe was used to being in the saddle. When we descended a very steep rocky slope, I was ready to get off and walk, but ahead of me Joe just swayed from side to side as his horse picked its way down.

We rode down to a dry creek bed of patterned meta-granite. White, pink, and gray rocks swirled and flowed together in the lengthening shadows of dusk. Growing around the creek edges were mesquite and creosote bushes. The horses took swipes at the mesquite and stalks of dry grass, but turned their noses up at the creosote.

We continued on to Sam's Point, a high spot where we could catch the sinking orange sun, glowing through and around the outstretched saguaro arms, and see desert cottontails hopping all around.

* * *

Tanque Verde is facing the same pressures that Lazy K Bar faces, but within the ownership there is a microcosm of the conflict and difference of opinions that exists in the larger urban arena. Bob Cote sees development as a fact of life. His business is well established and he believes it will continue to prosper even if they do away with the horseback riding. He doesn't feel the need to restrict people from moving into the area. On the topic of water, he believes there is enough for everyone, it just requires educating people on conservation techniques.

His wife, Leslie, on the other hand, worries about the continued growth in population and the effect it will have on the remaining natural areas and wildlife. She would like to see more restrictions placed on spreading development. She recognizes the impact

26

that the natural areas have on their business; their naturalist program has "gotten more positive response . . . than any other thing at the ranch."

BIRD BANDING — Mike Link

Tanque Verde Ranch has two distinctive wildlife habitats. There is the desert scrub of saguaro, palo verde, and mesquite, and there is the riparian (wet border) zone of cottonwoods, mesquite, seep willow, and salt cedar near a pond. In the desert, water attracts life; and in ecology a basic lesson is that the greatest concentration of species occurs along an edge, a border between natural communities.

Chuck Corchran wandered south like so many snowbirds from Minnesota, and became intrigued with the ranch, but not for riding. This retired bird bander observed a terrific opportunity. He approached the Cotes for permission to set up mist nets and to band birds.

Mist nets are fine-meshed nets that are invisible to a flying bird. The bird strikes the net, which has some give to it, and becomes entrapped. The banders then retrieve the captured bird, measure it, attach a leg band, and release it.

The project began as a once-a-week activity in the winter, but it soon grew to a year-around event. Chuck was joined by Donald Lamm, a retired Foreign Service employee.

As a young man, Don had been interested in museum work, but the Depression left no funds for field work, so he searched around for a job that would allow him to pursue his love of ornithology. The result of his career search was the Foreign Service. He put in requests for all the most exotic birding locations, places that did not have field guides. While serving in Australia, he listed three other posts that he was interested in transferring to. His choices were so unusual that his chief sent a personal letter asking him if he was sure that these were the posts he wanted. The letter added, "If you are, what strange birds are down there, and does Freddy [Don's wife] agree?"

Don helped write the monograph "Birds of Mozambique," and even had one bird named after him. He came to Tucson after retirement in 1966 and looked around for bird people.

Chuck had just gotten attention for having in his nets a black-capped vireo, an extremely rare bird that is normally found only in Mexico and a few sites in Texas. Don heard of this and became so excited that he quickly signed on for the banding project. Don reflected twelve years later, "It turned out to be the only black-capped vireo ever caught, and Charlie was so new [to the business] that he didn't even know that it was rare."

Later, they were joined by Phil Walters (a Ph.D. chemist) and his wife, Jori, from southern Illinois. Now the project attracts strangers, the curious, and bird-watchers who want to see what treasures they have caught.

Like all researchers, these people have a drive. They are a cohesive team of rather polished efficiency. Their conversation comes in a series of numbers that include band, American Ornithological Union number, age, sex, method of aging, wing measurement, weight, and molt. The birds are handled deftly, and released quickly.

They have enlivened the experience of ranch guests, and they have gotten the ranch to put out fifty-eight bird feeders so that guests can see the birds on the wing. On a more scientific basis, they have been able to add longevity records on western birds to our collective knowledge — the literature on western birds has always been slim. For example, they have recaptured elf owls and Lucy warblers that were known to be more than six years old.

There have been small adventures, like the time a rare female hooded merganser landed in the pond. Some banders went around the pond, which flushed the bird right into the net. "The bird was looking over its shoulder or it never would have hit the net." Charlie charged right into the water to retrieve the duck before it broke loose.

They have had other rarities too. Some sound like a checklist for eastern forests — ovenbird, hooded warbler, northern and Louisiana waterthrush, and rose-breasted grosbeak. Others have been Mexican immigrants, like the rufous-backed robin. But Charlie reflects, "If I had to pick one bird — the elf owl would be it. It's hard to believe, but they weigh only an ounce and a half."

It was our good fortune to see an elf owl sitting in the pot that they use for weighing birds. Turn your field guide to "owls"; the elf owl resembles the much bigger predators that most of us are familiar with. But set your book upright on the table, and an elf owl would be substantially shorter. A full-sized bird would fit on the page, with room for other illustrations. It is the world's smallest owl, but it is still a predator.

The elf owl lives in cavities and is most commonly associated with saguaro cactus, where it takes advantage of gila woodpecker holes for nests and protection. However, this is the most abundant owl in Arizona and it will roost in oaks, sycamores, and other trees as well.

For me, the Lucy warblers, chats, and other birds that they handled were all exciting. This was a special opportunity to really see the birds I have stalked so intently with my binoculars. But most impressive was the tiny elf owl, with its fifteen-inch wingspan.

It's little wonder that Charlie has devoted twenty years to this project despite the fact that he and his partners have never been employed by the ranch. They are working for the love of feathered critters.

JERRY BREWER, NATURALIST — Mike Link

All around us were the plants and animals of the eastern half of Saguaro National Monument. We were on the hot lower slopes, but we could see the darker shades of forests, where winter snows and tempera-

A brown towhee and bird-bander eye one another at the Tanque Verde Ranch. (K. Crowley)

Western diamondback rattlesnake. (G. Huey)

tures encourage northern spruce trees. Near the trail was a crepe flower, which dries out like the paper it is named for, and in the elevations above us were birds collecting pinecone nuts.

This was a naturalist's holiday, the two of us walking, sharing, speculating. The Englishman accompanying us was absorbing what he could in a land that will never know fog, the likes of which his home country thrives on.

Our guide was Jerry Brewer, naturalist, ex-professional baseball player, Vietnam vet, movie stuntman for horror flicks that need venomous animals, and herpetologist. He was born in Arkansas, lived in southern California, and is proud of his Indian heritage.

"I brought my first snake home when I was three. During my youth, the neighborhood called me 'bug boy.' I always had a net and jar with me.

"I can't tell you how many times I was kicked out of the house. 'Get in there and get them goddamn snakes out of your room. Pack your bags and get the hell out of here. It's either going to be you or the snakes.' "

On a walk on the Tanque Verde Ranch, Jerry meandered through the cactus and shrubs, probing, observing, sharing his knowledge and his philosophy.

"Ponderosa pine grew here twenty thousand years ago, but now this is Arizona, the arid zone. Only the Australian Outback has more ultraviolet light penetration than this area. Plants here make their carbon/oxygen exchange at night. They have thorns and needles so that hot liquids can move into them and be cooled by the winds. This keeps the plants from cooking themselves.

"Barrel cactus have novas [circles of growth] that concentrate at the top and face south like a compass. The accordion shape of the saguaros not only expands and contracts with addition and subtraction of moisture, it also produces shade.

"The creosote plant drops acidic material on the ground, which helps it to dominate other competitors. Creosote is the oldest living unchanged plant in the world. It evolved early.

"An eighteen hole golf course in the desert uses one million gallons of water per day!"

We wandered by a white-throated bush rat's mound, which was a combination of branches and horse dung in a three-foot-diameter circle. We also walked through a wash of stratified sand and gneiss—a combination of ancient geologic stress and recent erosion and deposition. There were never any glaciers here; the land was shaped by shelf movement, shifting, expansion, and contraction. Big pictures, little stories, tectonic changes, bushrat rearrangements.

Everything is visible in one way or another. The stories are waiting for the naturalists.

We considered the special life forms that dominate this area. The antelope ground squirrel can tolerate an internal temperature of 123 degrees, the highest of any mammal. Where rodents forage for seeds, they disturb the dry desert ground and provide a dusting area for birds.

The kangaroo rat (which is neither a rat nor a mouse, but a member of a different order of rodents) does not have to drink water. It metabolizes its food, converting starch into hydrocarbons, then hydrogen, which combines with the oxygen it breathes to form water. Its nasal membranes catch water before it can be removed by exhalation. The kangaroo rat doesn't urinate; instead it passes a pellet, which it also recycles once by swallowing, to minimize water loss. It has a gland that produces oil to keep its skin lubricated; and in captivity, if it is not furnished with sand, its pelage will be moist looking. The kangaroo rat's burrow has a higher humidity than the air at the surface, and through prolonged periods in the burrow, the animal gains moisture in its lungs.

When we discussed reptiles, Jerry really became animated. I have known many herpetologists over the years, and all of them are eccentric. All of them are emotional about their special corner of the animal world. While others cringe and display disgust, the herpetologists see beauty in form and design. They see the subtle shadings, the complex camouflage, the unique adaptations; and they see into a world of great secrecy.

A zebra-tailed lizard waved its tail to distract our attention. In case we wanted to eat the lizard, its ploy should leave us with only a writhing tail to crunch. A western whiptail scooted across the path, and we found the dropping of a regal horned lizard.

All naturalists are scatologists. Scats, droppings, turds—there are almost as many words as there are defecators. But the reason humans dissect these remnant spoor is because they tell so much about the animal—who, when, what it ate. It holds as much information as a little book.

A lizard pellet was something new for me, and the regal horned lizard's is perhaps the most spectacular. This was two inches by one-half inch (almost the equivalent of laying an egg) and rusty red. When we broke it apart, it crumbled into hundreds of ant heads—just heads. The regal eats around four hundred ants a day.

I asked Jerry about the gila monster, the only venomous lizard in the United States, and he was good for another story. "I work with about ten thousand venomous animals around the world and never get bit. I am a world authority on venomous animals, and I get bit by one of the slowest. It was embarrassing.

"This gila was in a development area, so I wanted to move it to someplace where it would be safe. It was a thirteen-inch specimen, so I brought it home first to show my family before I placed it in its new territory.

"My daughter was playing with the garden hose when I got home, and my neighbor came over. 'Jerry, those things are really fast, aren't they?'

"I wanted to show the neighbor how safe they are, so I took the lizard out of the box and set it down. 'See how it moves very slowly? It is quick only left and right, not straight ahead,' I said to the neighbor.

"My daughter came around the corner on a run to give me a hug. We collided and she knocked me off balance. She didn't know where the lizard was and started around me, so I put out my hand to block her. She pushed against me and I fell forward, put my right hand down to catch my fall, and placed my thumb right in front of the gila monster. That's what it grabbed."

The gila has an exceedingly strong grip with its mouth, and it introduces its venom through capillary action that brings the venom from the lower jaw through a grooved tooth. This is a slower process than the injection method of fanged reptiles, so the gila doesn't just strike and retreat, but hangs on with its powerful jaws. The bite produces intense burning, and free-flowing blood squirting from the wound. The anticoagulant that is injected prevents clotting.

Jerry shook his arm four times to dislodge the gila. Thirteen teeth were left embedded in his thumb.

Jerry experienced terrible pain, a burning sensation, and great swelling. The pain went up his arm past the elbow, and he felt chest pains too. His hand became so large that it seemed the skin would split. He didn't go to the hospital because, as he explained, "They would have called me for advice and I was already here." There is no antivenom for the gila bite.

Since no detailed medical descriptions of a gila bite and its effects on humans had been done, Jerry decided to contribute his experience. He described his fourteen hour ordeal into a tape recorder, and he called a photographer to record it visually.

* * *

Growing up, Jerry had encouragement in his herpetological interests. He worked as a volunteer for the old Los Angeles Zoo when he was just a kid. He rode his bike to the zoo, where he would do any odd jobs. What caught the attention of the zoo keepers was the fact that he always brought fresh vegetables. He didn't like the junk that the visitors were bringing for the animals to eat. As he got older, he got to clean stalls and use the library.

In addition, two herpetologists took him under their wings and encouraged him to learn the Latin names so that he could communicate with professionals all over the world. His career odyssey then took him to the jungles of Vietnam, with an intermediary period as a professional ballplayer for the Los Angeles Dodgers system. While in the military he became an automatic weapons specialist, but the weapon he was most familiar with was a "nocturnal, heat-seeking, spring-loaded, chemo-receptive, hypodermic nee-

A pair of antelope ground squirrels are alert and poised for action if danger threatens. These small desert mammals can tolerate internal temperatures of 123 degrees Fahrenheit. (J. Honcoop)

dle," or rattlesnake.

Jerry was wounded in action and sent to a hospital. It was there that he became a venomous snake consultant. "There was a kid a few beds down from me and these doctors kept going down there everyday and they'd walk away shaking their heads. Finally I got out of bed and walked down there and looked at him. He had all this edema and ecchymosis and blebs [blisters] all over his face.

"I looked him over and said, 'Boy that's a real nasty green tree viper bite. Did you happen to be a point man?' 'Ya.' 'You were walking through the bushes and all of a sudden, boom, your face started burning and swelling?' 'Ya.'

"Then the doctors walked up and said, 'Hey, what are you doing here next to the patient?' I said, 'I'm just looking at this green tree viper bite.'"

They were happy to have a mystery solved, and Jerry was now a consultant to the military on venomous bites.

His career after the service included a stint with the Los Angeles Zoo as a keeper (during which he acquired a polar bear bite), work with the Fish and Wildlife Service, research, acting, and even a position as manager of a pest control service. Part-time, he was a naturalist at Tanque Verde, movie extra, and consultant to the hospital and military. But a combination of part-time positions is seldom enough to keep a person going, and when the ranch offered him a full-time job, he happily accepted.

"Nature to me is my life. When the alarm goes off, I'm ready to go, because I'm going to see beautiful things and have a good time.

"My dad always told me, 'Go out and get a decent job because those snakes are never going to put bread and butter on your table. All those damn things are going to do is bite you and kill you.'

"Now, of course, my parents are proud of me. I have just been an animal person all my life, especially venomous animals."

And venomous animals are part of the mystique of the desert. There is a saying that everything in the desert stings, bites, or wears thorns. That is an exaggeration, but it is also a fascination. Jerry likes to tell stories, and people like to hear about his adventures.

He can tell you about a sidewinder that got away from him at home. It crawled into a vent and into his wall. For five weeks it would rattle every time someone tapped on the wall. Finally, he used ammonia to get it out. He can also tell you about crawling under a trailer home to remove a snake, and finding it coiled and ready to strike right next to the hole in the skirting that he had crawled through.

But there is a serious side to Jerry, the herpetologist,

Zebra-tailed lizard. (G. Huey)

naturalist, educator. He deals with the myths that still abound in the area. There are stories of extra-lethal snakes that are caused by hybridization, but he knows that in the lab, the venom does not show this. One story had a rattler and king snake interbreeding to make a supersnake. Since one is oviparous (egg laying) and the other is viviparous (live bearing), the hybridization is biologically impossible.

People talk about aggressive snakes, but Jerry will tell you, "That mechanism in his mouth is for catching prey after dark. It is an offensive weapon, not a defensive. The snake does not want to bite you."

Jerry will quickly point out that ninety-seven percent of all snakebite victims are males between the ages of thirteen and thirty, and most are trying to manipulate the snake. Most of these events are also associated with drugs or alcohol. In the United States, there are 3,800 bites annually (on the average) and only 12 fatalities. In Arizona, the numbers are 108 and 2. By comparison, more than 200 people a year die from bee, wasp, or hornet stings.

"If I can get people that come here to appreciate snakes so that they don't kill the next one they see crossing the road or their path, I will have accomplished something."

But while Jerry affects those who listen, he knows the fight for understanding of reptiles has a long way to go. He still has to battle those who are charged with the snake's protection. He knows that game people aren't necessarily snake people, that bird watchers are not necessarily snake watchers, even though birds and snakes are evolutionarily near one another. Judges that will defend other endangered species may not be as quick to protect the snake.

"Too often," Jerry says, "Humans think all of nature out here is for their enjoyment, to dispose of, like food in grocery stores, like cattle that are butchered for our tables. I just can't see going out and killing natural animals when it is not needed. They should be observed and watched closely. If it were up to me there would be no hunting unless you did it with a camera.

"What chose me to be a human instead of another animal? Would I want something stalking me for my hide?

"I don't mind people visiting here. I just don't want them to move here. We have to stop promoting growth. With growth you have habitat destruction."

Jerry wants to educate people on the beauty of nature. Awareness, respect, and appreciation are the keys for him. "I want to get people to look at something closely and respect it as life. Death gives to life in ecology. There is no real grief out there until man interferes."

31

San Xavier del Bac Mission. (D. Dietrich)

THE MISSION TRAIL

BY KATE CROWLEY

Tumacacori, San Xavier del Bac, and Los Santos Angeles de Guevavi, three early Jesuit missions, were established in the late sixteenth and early seventeenth centuries. All three have seen rebellion, Apache raids, Jesuits and Franciscans, abandonment, and varying degrees of restoration. Guevavi has fared the least well of the three. It is located closest to the Mexican border, on private land, and has very nearly been reclaimed by the surrounding desert.

Over the centuries the Arizona desert has seen and absorbed countless explorers and inhabitants. The earliest people traveled in small groups and adapted to the ways of the land. They lived simply, and moved on when their needs could no longer be met in one place. It was a hostile environment, and there were other aggressive nomadic people to avoid.

In the late 1500s, the area now known as northwestern Mexico became the new frontier for Spanish explorers. They called the land New Spain, and together the cavalry and the Jesuit missionaries introduced European culture and religion to the Indian people. Like present-day missionaries, they felt they were doing God's work in bringing the Christian message, along with humanitarian help, to those "less fortunate" than themselves.

One man in particular stands out in the history of these missionary settlements, the Italian Jesuit Father Eusabio Francisco Kino. Born in 1645, he joined the Jesuit order after recovering from a serious illness — he had prayed to Saint Francis Xavier, the founder of the Society of Jesus (Jesuits) for intercession. His missionary travels eventually put him in the land of the Pima Indians, where he vigorously worked to teach the people improved farming techniques and to build communities around the mission churches.

The Pimas were a peaceful people who already had a basic farming culture. Their willingness to accept the white people's religion caused resentment on the part of the traditional Indian spiritual leaders, which led to an uprising in 1695.

Father Kino also worked to develop cooperation among the various Piman groups so that they could provide a unified defense against their aggressive long-time neighbors, the Apaches. By 1692, Father Kino was establishing a more peaceful and secure existence for the Pimas, and when the 1695 uprising was brutally put down by the Spanish troops, it was left to Father Kino to restore the confidence of the people who had trusted in him and his ways of peace.

Preceding Father Kino had been Father Daniel Marras, whose willingness to work with the people won him admiration and support. In his efforts to improve the Indians' lives, he managed to increase six hundred head of cattle to a herd of more than fifty thousand. The combination of cattle grazing and permanent settlements began a chain of human ecological impacts.

The first half of the 1700s saw the Jesuits' continued efforts to expand the faith and improve the Indians' lives. But with the discovery of a massive silver mine, mining camps sprung up among the Indian pueblos; and dissatisfaction, hatred, and greed worked together to create the setting for another rebellion.

In 1767, Charles III of Spain banished the Jesuits from the entire Spanish empire, and the Franciscans entered to fill the vacant niche. Beginning in the 1780s and lasting for a short period of forty years, the mission complex flowered once again.

The Apaches were actively terrorizing the northern frontier, economic decline was putting pressure on the dependent missions, and in Europe Napoleon was sweeping across Spain, ending its colonial hold on the new world. With Mexico's independence in 1821, the missions were deserted and left to be reclaimed by the wind, sun, and rain.

There are just two remaining missions, San Xavier del Bac and Tumacacori, both preserved so that people today are able to experience that time when Arizona was shared by the seekers of gold and the seekers of souls.

Tumacacori National Monument. (E. Cooper)

In 1700, Father Kino laid the foundation of the beautiful San Xavier del Bac near the largest of the Pima villages that bordered the Santa Cruz River. Its great distance from the protection of Spanish forces kept it virtually empty until 1740. Kino had hoped to make his headquarters here, but an inability to find replacements for himself at his missions to the south made the move impossible.

Through the years, the mission church sustained repeated damage and rebuilding. The structure that exists now was built in 1797. When Arizona became a part of the United States in 1853, San Xavier's future brightened. Its proximity to Tucson meant it would receive church, state, and federal assistance, assuring its preservation.

San Xavier is the perfect image of a Southwest mission church, the white-washed adobe walls contrasting with the deep-blue desert sky. It is easy to understand the effect of such a shining, intricately carved temple on the people who lived with simple patterns and earth colors. Statues of saints and angels fill numerous crevices and corners, while rows of blazing votive candles flicker in colored glass containers below. In one alcove rests the life-size statue of a dead Saint Xavier. Pinned to a blanket that covers the statue are numerous hospital bracelets and gold charms, petitions and thank-yous from the faithful for cures and favors. Even today, there remains a mix of the old beliefs with the "new."

San Xavier del Bac is a functioning Catholic church, with daily Mass serving tourists as well as the local Indians.

* * *

After a visit to the cool mountain forests of Madera Canyon, we drove down to the flat, hot lowlands and headed towards Tumacacori.

As I walked out of the cool, dark National Park Service exhibit area into the blinding midday sun, my eyes hurt and I could almost feel a headache start while I fumbled for the sunglasses hanging around my neck.

It was quiet at this time of day, and the most noticeable activity was the little lizards that zipped across the path, with my son in hot pursuit. As I looked around at the dry land and the crumbling adobe ruins of Tumacacori, I tried to envision the lives of the Indians and the missionaries who once worked together to create a community.

There are no pews, no elaborate paintings or statuary in this sanctuary. If you look closely, you can see some faint colors on the adobe walls, but that is all the decoration that is left.

In the compound there are low adobe brick walls outlining the courtyard, rooms where the priests lived, storerooms, workshops, granaries, and classrooms that made up the social and agricultural foundation of the community.

Gardens and an orchard used to grow within the courtyard walls. There were cisterns with connecting drains, and to the north of the church, a cemetery for the Christian Indians. Over the years, the cemetery has fallen victim to wandering cattle, weather, and vandalizing treasure hunters, so that nothing remains of the original burial mounds.

Back inside the main building that houses the museum and park offices, I wandered out into a lush garden. Water trickled with a soothing sound from a small fountain into a clear pool. In the trees and on the garden walls, the grackles kept up a noisy squawking chatter, but it was still easy to relax on the stone retainers and breathe in the lush smells of earth and green plants, many of which were identified by common and Latin names.

While the ancient prophets may have gone into the desert to meditate and pray, I would always choose a garden like this one to contemplate the mysteries.

Between the two missions, I much preferred the quiet, introspective qualities of Tumacacori. I was able to see the past and wonder about the future. What will this dry desert land look like in two centuries? The sun and sand and cactus and lizard have forged a delicate balance through the ages. Will we continue to allow expansion into an environment that demands our restraint for its survival?

Crumbling cavalry barracks stand like silent sentinels at Fort Bowie National Monument. (D. Dietrich)

THE OLD WEST

FORT BOWIE — Kate Crowley

When you arrive at Fort Bowie National Historic Site, you find yourself in a parking lot surrounded by dry brown hills, with rockier peaks looming beyond. There are no buildings other than a solar-powered outhouse. The old fort is nowhere in sight.

The area quickly gives the feeling of an earlier time, a dangerous time, when the ever-westward-flowing settlers faced very poor odds of survival if they chose to homestead in this region.

It is a quiet place, the only sounds are the wind flowing down from the hills and whispering through the dry grass and leaves, and a few birds squeaking or chirping in the shrubs.

The only way for visitors to reach the ruins of the old fort is on foot, up a one-and-a-half-mile trail that begins midway in Apache Pass. It would not be a pleasant hike in the middle of summer, when temperatures can easily reach one hundred degrees.

Because of the fort's remote location and difficult access, it is not surprising to learn that annual visitation runs around seven thousand. But for those who want to experience the feeling of isolation and suspense that confronted soldiers and travelers on the Butterfield Stage line as they attempted to negotiate the pass, it is an appropriate way to maintain the national historic site.

The ancient rocks were for two or three centuries the sheltering abode of the Apaches. Originally from the northern Athabaskan-speaking tribes, the Apaches moved into the Southwest, pushing less aggressive peoples aside and earning the Zuni title *apachu*, which means "enemy."

The Apaches knew the land intimately. They were capable of subsisting on meager amounts of food and water, moving as the game and harvest, or enemies, dictated. It was not an easy life, but it was self-determined and free.

The Apaches were traditional enemies of the Mexicans. Raids to take livestock and goods were an in-tegral part of Apache culture. A mutual hatred for one another led to killings on both sides.

The Butterfield Stage route began in 1857 as a mail route from Tipton, Missouri, to San Francisco, California. A spring at Apache Pass was the only source of reliable water between the San Simon River and Ewell's Station, southwest of the Dos Cabezas range. A stage station was constructed of stone in the valley west of the spring in 1858.

A man by the name of James Tevis ran the station in the late 1850s, and he knew the legendary Apache chief Cochise. Living there without threats from the Indians, he confidently dug a well, built a hotel, and later planted orchards in Bowie, which was approximately fifteen miles north of the pass, to accomodate the Southern Pacific Railroad.

All went smoothly until 1861, when a boy was kidnapped from a ranch in the Patagonia-Sonoita region. The blame was put on Cochise, and a detachment from Fort Buchanan was sent to recover the boy and bring the culprit to justice. A young Lieutenant George Bascom was put in charge of the search party. He went to the Apache Pass station and arranged a meeting with Cochise. Unsuspecting and innocent, the chief was accused of the crime, which he denied. Bascom intended to hold him until the boy was returned, but Cochise escaped from his would-be captors by cutting a hole in the tent wall and retreating into the hills he knew so well.

Over the next sixteen days more hostages were taken on both sides, and the trouble reached a boiling point when the army hung six Indians who had accompanied Cochise to the meeting. The event, which came to be known as the Bascom Affair, touched off twelve years of war between the Chiricahua Apaches and American soldiers and settlers.

A major ambush and the Battle of Apache Pass, in mid-July 1862, led to the establishment of Fort Bowie. A group of eighteen hundred California Volunteers was on route to the Rio Grande to fight the Confederates when they were ambushed by several hundred Apaches. The Chiricahua, according to some, were the best guerrilla fighters of all the Indian nations, but they were unprepared for two mountain howitzers that Captain Thomas Roberts carried with him.

The big guns blasted the Indians from their rocky hiding places and sent them scattering for better cover. They regrouped and attacked again the next day, only to be met with more artillery fire.

General Carleton decided that the only way the pass would be kept open for military or civilian travelers was through the use of force, and within a month, a rudimentary Fort Bowie was established. The first fort was built by the Fifth California Volunteer Infantry in the dizzying heat of July. It consisted of low stone breastworks surrounding a cluster of canvas tents and a stone guardhouse.

As you wander along the narrow trail today, you can see the remnants of the small stage station in the scrubby vegetation. As you look at the uneven, faint, rocky route that served as a road for the stage, it is hard to comprehend people willingly choosing to venture into that uncertain land.

Having grown up with westerns on the big screen and TV, I could close my eyes and easily hear the rattle of harnesses, the snap of a whip, and the creak of an old wooden coach as it leaves the station.

Walking further up the trail, closer to the spring, I felt a vague sense of unease begin to build. There are trees and rocks all around that could easily conceal an attacker. Again the movie scene erupts in my mind, and I hear the air slice as an imaginary arrow pierces a tree branch beside me. I feel the anxiety that the soldiers must have known as they made their way up this pass.

These Hollywood images contrast with the surroundings: the life-giving spring, and the beautiful hills all around. I can understand the frustration and anger that the Indian people must have felt as they watched intruders come in and usurp this essential valley.

After the Bascom Affair, there was one white man who was able to gain the trust and faith of Cochise. His name was Thomas Jeffords, and his story has been popularized in the book *Blood Brother* and the film *Broken Arrow* (later also a TV series), which glamorized and fictionalized the truth of these men's lives. They were exceptional men, who could accept one another as individuals, with differing backgrounds but common goals.

Jeffords was superintendent of the mail between Tucson and Fort Bowie, but after the Bascom Affair, many of his mail riders were losing their lives in their attempts to deliver the mail sacks. Through sheer personal courage and possibly some naivete, Jeffords rode out to the Pinaleño (Graham) Mountains, was met by Apache warriors, gave them his guns, and said he wanted to talk to Cochise. He knew how to speak some Athabaskan, and was able to convince Cochise

that his riders were not carrying military correspondence. He asked that they be allowed to pass freely.

Cochise was very impressed by Jefford's courage and honesty, and agreed to protect the mail riders. The mutual respect the two men had for one another grew into a close friendship that lasted until Cochise's death in 1874. Tom Jeffords was with Cochise just before he died, and he was the only white man to know where the great chief was buried, east of his treasured stronghold. When Jeffords died, the secret went with him.

In 1868, construction of the "permanent" Fort Bowie began on a plateau to the east of the original site. While Cochise and Geronimo were still at large and attacking, the post served as a base for campaigns to subdue the rebellious Indians. Cochise and General Oliver Howard made peace in 1872, through the intercession of Tom Jeffords.

After the abolition of the reservation in 1876, Geronimo and his followers appeared and disappeared into the Sierra Madre Range until 1886, when they were all shipped to forts in Florida and Alabama.

Fort Bowie grew to encompass more than thirty-five structures, including storehouses, a hospital, a post trader's, and enlisted men's barracks. Most were made of adobe brick, but the officers' quarters were large houses built of wood, further up the plateau.

There was little to do at Fort Bowie, and the heat and isolation were oppressive. Beer, even warm beer, was a valued commodity.

The fort was officially abandoned in 1894. It wasn't long before the buildings were dismantled by locals who coveted the free wood, and the remaining adobe walls have gradually shrunk under years of rain and wind.

To walk around the grounds today is to feel a mixture of sadness and disbelief. To build such a complete community high in the desert, hundreds of miles from major supply sources, was an ambitious and expensive undertaking, especially when you consider that it functioned for only thirty-two years.

FARAWAY RANCH—Mike Link

Beneath the rocky promontories, in a grassy valley with scattered juniper and yucca and a cottonwood creek, white-throated swifts do aerial reconnaissance. Grama grass grows in a volcanic soil with a mixture of deer droppings and prickle poppy. Acorn woodpeckers hammer on the rough bark of the alligator juniper, and a rock squirrel looks down from an isolated rhyolite tower. The cholla have flame-red flowers, and ash-throated flycatchers dart back and forth from their perches.

This is Faraway Ranch, a peaceful valley, a few buildings, and memories. It is in the lower reaches of Chiricahua National Monument, in the quiet zone before the visitor center and the campground. It is in a valley of subtle vistas and beauty, before the rock gardens that dominate the monument.

In 1888, Neil and Emma Erickson and their daughter Lillian moved from Fort Bowie to this land. They had one neighbor, J. Hu Stafford, who had settled there in 1886. Stafford, 45, and his 13-year-old bride lived in a small cabin near the creek. Stafford had stayed with a family in Salt Lake City, and found a stowaway in his wagon on his return trip. Being a practical man in a country without many opportunities, he married her, and the two of them raised fruit and vegetables to sell to the army at Fort Bowie. They also raised five children.

On a selling trip, he met Emma, and she became interested in the valley where the Staffords lived. Emma worked as a maid for an officer's wife and she knew too well the life that military men led. As a result, she purchased the home from Stafford and planned to move there when Neil was discharged.

Both Emma and Neil were immigrants. She came to the United States in 1873, Neil in 1879. Neil's father had preceded him to Minnesota and took work with the Northern Pacific Railroad for the construction of its western route. Along the way, the father disappeared, and blame was placed on Indians, even though there was no proof. Neil heard of this in Sweden, and came over to avenge his father's death.

He joined the army and said he would like to fight the Indians, but Minnesota was at peace, so he chose to go to the West. There he lost his desire for fighting as he came to realize that the Indians were fighting to protect their homeland. Neil fell in love with the land and sympathized with the Indian position.

Emma and Neil met at Fort Craig, and were both transferred to Fort Bowie. They were married in Tucson, and their first child, Lillian, was born at the fort before they settled in Bonita Canyon.

Faraway Ranch was founded as a cattle operation, but Neil had to make his living as a miner and carpenter in Bisbee, until he became the first forest ranger in the Chiricahua Forest Preserve. The ranch then became the Forest Service headquarters for his daily rounds in the adjacent wooded country.

Two more children were born, Louis Benton (Ben) and Hildegard. By 1899, Neil had added a living room, dining room, kitchen, and second-floor bedroom to the house to accomodate his growing family. In 1915, he put adobe around the old frame house and took out the cabin that had been the original home. In the practical manner of frontier expansion and carpentry, Neil took a simple picket log cabin, added a stone house, made a boxlike structure of mill-processed lumber, and expanded with adobe.

The home is now part of Chiricahua National Monument's interpretive program. The interior is decorated with original furnishings, and the fireplace is a monument that was built by the Tenth Cavalry in honor of President Garfield. This was a buffalo soldier unit, and the name of the first black graduate of West Point, H. O. Flipper, is one of the names on the stones. Neil wanted the government to preserve the monument, but they wouldn't, so he moved it into his home.

It was Lillian who took over the ranch. She married Ed Riggs of Sulphur Springs Valley, and together with Hildegard they operated the first "dude" ranch in Arizona. It was 1917 when Lillian suggested the guest-ranch idea. She saw so many people coming and staying with them that she decided it should be a business proposition. The first guests that came worked with the cattle and got involved with doing ranch duties as well as riding the horses.

By 1920, guests were picked up in Willcox and taken from the train to the ranch by automobile. Neil provided the storytelling that has become a trademark of all guest ranches, and the ranch grew to accomodate the guests.

In 1920, they added a swimming pool and planted persimmon, apple, pear, almond, and plum trees. The Stafford cabin was added as a guest accomodation, and the ranch had two hundred cattle and twenty guests. Neil and his horse, George, were celebrities, and Lillian was identified as the "Lady Boss of Faraway Ranch" in a *Saturday Evening Post* article.

Ed Riggs pushed for the creation of Chiricahua National Monument and the protection of the "wonderland of rocks." He built trails that took visitors into the maze of rock formations. Later, Ed would serve as trail boss for the CCC in establishing the monument's hiking trails.

Lillian lost her hearing when she was young, and lost her eyesight later, when she was bucked from a horse and hit her head. She continued to ride anyway. She was definitely the boss, dominating the guest ranch with her intense desire to learn, her religious faith, her strict management of staff, and her gracious manners with guests. She died in 1977, just as women everywhere were striving for the same independence that she found "far away."

GRAPEVINE RANCH — Mike Link

"Please DO NOT throw sticks or rocks for Patches, the black and white border collie, to fetch! She likes it, but it ruins her for working cattle, so be firm and resist!" Yup, the Old West continues, but like the dog's name, it is found in patches. The brochure for Grapevine Ranch describes two kinds of guest ranches, "a resort in a western setting" and "the primitive ranch." Grapevine is in the second category.

Eve and Gerry Searle own the ranch and are a big part of the experience. Eve describes Gerry like this: "He is first and foremost a horseman, then a cowboy and rancher. He's been with horses all his life, from about age four. He has ridden them, driven them, trained them, hated them, and loved them. There is nothing he doesn't know about them, and if he tells you that you can handle it, believe me, you can! Gerry can do lots of other things as well. He is an accomplished cowboy artist, and many of his paintings hang in various establishments in Tucson; he acted in western movies, doing mostly horse stunts; and he knows a great deal about cattle and the ranching industry. Another thing — he sure can spin a tale!"

Eve Searle whispers encouragement into the ear of one of the Grapevine Ranch trail horses. (K. Crowley)

To add to the color of the ranch, Eve has her own story to tell. "I came here from Europe via India, Mexico, and Australia (where I was a commercial pilot and flight instructor). When I arrived in Arizona, some fifteen years ago, I too fell in love with cattle and horses, and adopted the country way of life, farming and ranching."

Grapevine Canyon is one of the entry points for the Dragoon Mountains and the high rocky area that is known as Cochise Stronghold. The Dragoons are a small range with a granite core. The rocks are a jumble of joints, fractures, spalling, sheeting, and exfoliation formations that will not accept a footprint. They are the gates to vanishing, the land that Cochise used to hide his people and hold off the U.S. military. It was here that Tom Jeffords and Cochise planned peace, instead of war.

The canyon is named for the wild Arizona grapes that grow in the stream valley. They have large maplelike leaves and shreddy bark, and the juicy black fruits can be turned into pies, jelly, wine, and wildlife food. The ranch is blessed with water, a stream that runs ten months a year, and a surrounding greenstone ridge that holds the water in the valley. This was a *ciénaga*, a swamp, in the past. The waters invited early Indians to settle here. The Dragoon culture (which differs from both the Anasazi and the Hohokam) made camps near the valley and lived here until the fifteenth century, when either drought or Apaches (or both) drove them out.

Grapevine is a new ranch, one that follows in the footsteps of Mike Noonan (a tall Irishman with flaming red hair and beard), the three C's (Chiricahua Cattle Company), Cobre Loma Ranch, and the Hatley family ranch, which were also in the Dragoons. Grapevine was owned by Carl Adams, an illustrator from New York, before the Searles purchased it in 1982.

Gerry says, "There's too many modernized ways of doing things now. They aren't always the best." Modern ways don't suit Gerry, a rugged individualist who was born in Rice Lake, Wisconsin, worked farms in the Dakotas, ran a horse and cattle ranch in Montana, took work with the cowboy movies and television as a stunt rider, and worked cattle in Tucson before coming to the Dragoons. "There's a new breed of cowboy coming on the market. They have gone back to the old ways. In flatter country you don't need cowboys, you need ropers who can go out in ATVs and pickups. We like to do it the old way and we think it's easier on the calves."

Their ranch doesn't give one-hour rides, they don't take you loping—they saddle up and go for the whole day. "I keep these horses tuned up. People come here to relax, not to party. They come here and comment on the quiet."

Kate, Alyssa, and I took a ride with Gerry and two women, a geologist from Alberta and a medical assistant from Cincinnati. Our itinerary would take eight hours in the saddle, and we would cross a number of ridges, plunge down very steep slopes, and sample a lot of the landscape. Our trail went through juniper, mesquite, and manzanita in the wash, then up into agave, prickly pear, pincushion cactus, sycamore, and pinyon pine. Desert willows with purple and white trumpet-shaped flowers were thick in some parts of the creek.

Apache plume, a shrub of dry, rocky slopes and washes, has white flowers that resemble apple blossoms because of their size. The flowers produce feathery-tailed fruits that are greenish at first, but become tinged with red later on. They are called Apache plume because they are said to resemble an Indian feathered headdress. To me, they are ethereal in appearance, ghostlike, making me think of the spirits of the Apache that seem to travel in these canyons and draws.

We passed through the old town of Middlemarch, an old mine site, and a campground. There were storm clouds above the peaks and one bolt of lightning crashed in the distance, but the sky above was bright blue. A wind blew across our backs and threatened to steal our hats. Maggie, the sheep dog, guided us through the ravines and over the ridges with her tongue hanging out.

The trails down were white-knuckled for some of the group. Occasionally, I could see a tight grip on a saddle horn and eyes shut in quick and quiet prayer, but the horses had steady strides and could handle the descent better than their riders. Give the horse its lead, check it on flat spots, and let it go on the steep.

On the trail, Gerry reminded everyone, "We don't cut you no slack here. I change the horses around and make 'em perform. It's like a kid. You let them do everything they want to do and they'll get in trouble. Sometimes you got to thump 'em a little."

"Lots of people think I'm mean to my horses. I am not mean. I expect discipline, response, whatever, and if I don't get 'em, I'll thump 'em."

It soon becomes apparent that Gerry really does know horses, and he certainly isn't mean. These are not trail horses that ride along with their noses in the next mount's butt. They are good horses with their personalities intact.

Gerry isn't opposed to telling the rider how to ride better, either. He is direct and minces no words, but while he may take a rider off a horse, he won't thump the rider. "When you get on that horse, I want you to ride my way. I don't want anybody hurt."

His gruffness is part of his charm. He fits our image of the cowhand, riding tall in the saddle, leaning against a tree and rolling a cigarette, strapping on his sixgun, and spinning a yarn in his favorite chair by the lodge fireplace. "Wranglers are a dime a dozen. They all wear a belt buckle about this big around, a big hat, and a pair of boots. But they don't know beans and

buckshot about a horse. That's not true about all, but there are very few exceptions.

"A wrangler can't be a good wrangler unless he thinks. Thinking about the condition of the horse—how everything fits on the horse, the terrain, the kind of riders he has. It's not a simple job, it's time consuming. It demands positioning so that you can watch and evaluate your guests. You have to be there when it's necessary and that means anticipating. You have to know what you can do."

My horse was called Smoky. It was a large and dark gray, seemed rather mild-mannered, and had a history of being easygoing. We had no trouble getting along throughout the first half of our ride. The only hesitation that the horse showed was near the water hole, where it shied away and would not drink, but that presented no problem for me.

We stopped for lunch in the bottom of the canyon and rested our backs against some trees, where we talked about life, horses, and ranches. "My brother said, 'You know, you guys are like me. There's no way you can retire. We've worked all our life, if we sit down for a few days, we get so damn stiff we can't hardly move. We have to keep going.' I thought that was a hell of a thing to say."

Between the years of Faraway Ranch and Grapevine there was a time when this was the dude ranch capital of the country, but most ranches were squeezed out by a combination of insurance premiums, poor management, and not enough working capital. There are lots of unpredictable parts to ranching. Like my horse, Smoky. Shortly after lunch, Gerry told me to hold up with the last three horses, while the first three worked their way up a steep grade. I said, "Sure," and waited.

As soon as the first horses started to go, mine wanted to move. I said no and made him wait. His posture and ears told me he was peeved. Then Gerry said, "Come on," and I gave the horse the okay. It did not move. I gave it a little heel, and a voice command. It stiffened its legs, becoming absolutely rigid, and its ears came all the way back. I knew it was time to get off or pay the price, so I took Gerry's advice and stuck 'em. The horse sucked in air, dropped its head, and started to buck. I reined his head in beside his front haunches, so he couldn't really get bucking. Instead, he spun, and I found myself facing Kate and another woman on a trail that had room for only one horse at a time. I kept the horse reined in to spin it away from them. The horse either decided to roll or took a misstep on the granite boulders, and we went over into the wash.

It was lucky that I sensed the fall and was able to rise up in the saddle and step off as it crashed to the ground, because the horse thrashed like a tantrum-throwing child and would have ground my leg to mush.

Gerry came charging down the steep grade in full control of his horse and got everything calmed down. I walked the horse a while and then got on and rode

IN MEMORY
OF
LITTLE ROBE
SON OF
GERONIMO
APACHE CHIEF
Died
Sept. 10 1885
Age two years

The Apache Indians fought the U.S. Army for years to retain their traditional lands. Many died on both sides. Today the wind and cactus are the companions for Geronimo's young son, buried at Fort Bowie National Monument. (K. Crowley)

42

him the rest of the day without incident.

Gerry walks with a limp and I asked him why. "Horse fell off a mountain and rolled over three or four times." Gerry "went out the front door the full length of the reins," but he would not let go. Horse and rider rolled over and over, but Gerry got right back on. He wasn't about to walk back.

"I'll tell you what—it takes a little longer to get healed up now."

The Plains Indians said that the great spirit created horses to make the scenery more beautiful. It is the one domestic animal that seems to belong in wild country. Wild horse herds are not natural in the United States, even though they evolved on this continent. There was a period of hundreds of thousands of years when they were not in the Americas, until the Spanish brought them back through Central and South America. Now they are part of the land's mystique, and they have a special significance to horse lovers, like birds do to birders.

Eve has written, "I have always loved horses, and when I was a little girl, I was so besotted about them that my governess, tucking me into bed at night, on a couple of occasions, sighed: 'Child, child, one day you'll wake up and you'll have turned into a horse!' What she meant as a threat, I took as a promise. Every morning I would wake up and hurriedly feel my face to see if a long horsey nose was in place of the clothes peg I had put there the night before (to improve its shape)—but no luck, it never happened. I think that was one of the major disappointments of my early life. I learned to run like a horse, leading with one leg and then the other, I learned to twitch my ears, I even, to my mother's horror, pawed the ground and foamed at the mouth, but the anticipated transformation eluded me."

* * *

Arizona is a land of seasons, but seasons are defined in different ways by the people of the north, where the winter snow, spring flowers, green summer, and colorful fall leaves mark the divisions. In the desert, spring is a time to move the cattle and it is a time of flowering and bird song; fall is also time to move the cattle to a different grazing range. Winter is dry, and summer is the rainy season. It is hotter in summer, and might be unbearable, but it is cooled by regular mid-day rains.

This is how Eve describes one rainy summer: "Wonderful rain we've had so far this summer, the first monsoon in a year that seems to me to be normal. It came on time, and it's soaking us with the required amounts of the good stuff almost daily. For those out there who immediately think that we are sitting under dripping, leaden skies (the way your rain works), let me tell you, not so, the desert rains are different. Mostly the days begin sunny, perhaps with a little cloud, then about the time you think nothing's going to happen, Bingo! The most magnificent lightning storm begins, with spectacular fireworks and booming thunder . . . and then, on a lucky day, the downpour . . . .

"The countryside has responded magnificently. The range is covered with fresh new grass, the cows are smiling, the mesquite trees are lush and loaded with beans, providing feasts for the horses, who trail lazily from tree to tree, tasting a bit here and a bit there."

Guests join in cattle drives, and explore hidden trails. That's the life of Grapevine Ranch. "There's nothing in the world dumber than a cowboy. There's no other man living that would go out and abuse himself on a horse in the brush, get run over, get bucked off, work long hours at fifty cents an hour, except a dumb cowboy," says Gerry. "And that's damn near the whole truth, but I like it, I really wouldn't want to do anything else."

CHARACTERS OF THE LAND

A DESERT SETTING — Mike Link

From Willcox, a playa sweeps south between the Dos Cabezas and the Dragoon Mountains. Sulphur Springs Valley continues south beside the Chiricahua, Swisshelm, and Pedregosa Mountains, and the lowlands swing southwest to the Mule Mountains at Bisbee. The playa is the deepest part of ancient Lake Cochise, which was a twenty-mile-long lake in the Pleistocene time.

The playa is the lowest place in the landscape, the collecting reservoir for all the runoff of the neighboring mountains. It is an alkali basin, a mix of calcium, sodium, and potassium carbonates that have leeched from the surrounding rocks and soil and accumulated here as the waters fill the shallow basin and then evaporate. The result is a salt-white valley floor that shimmers in the summer sunlight.

Parallel with Sulphur Springs Valley is the San Pedro River Valley, which is dominated by a river flowing north from Mexico. Both valleys are part of the Chihuahuan desert, a shrubby desert with much less bird life and cactus growth than the Sonoran. Frederich Gehlbach says that only three to thirteen species of birds will nest in a shrub desert community; if the area is dissected with an arroyo, you can expect eleven to sixteen. The verdin, finch, and crissal thrasher are the most abundant birds.

Tarbush, a small shrub with a yellow nodding flower that cattle find bitter and unpalatable, grows with sandpaper bush and Chihuahuan white thorn, shrubs that dominate the Chihuahuan zone. However, if one plant had to be the symbol for the area, it would be the creosote bush.

The plant has bright yellow flowers, which are followed by white fuzzy seedballs. After a rain, the shrubs give off an odor you might be familiar with from freshly treated telephone poles. The Indians collected the resinous crusts from the branches to mend pots and to stick their arrowheads on wooden shafts. Only the black-throated sparrow regularly uses the creosote for its nest.

The Chihuahuan desert is higher than the Sonoran, and colder. Overall, there are more grassland complexes in this desert than in the Sonoran. The two meet in this area, surrounding the various mountain ranges with hostile environments for plant and animal movement.

The real bonanza for this area was not plant, nor animal, but mineral. The surrounding ranges contain lead, copper, zinc, turquoise, silver, and gold in their highly faulted and metamorphic hearts, and that meant wealth and boom.

This is basin and range country, an area of great crustal unrest, with faults, folds, and volcanic energy. Numerous mountain ranges have literally risen from the broad planes. This has been a mobile part of the earth's crust, where plate tectonics have exerted push and pull, and faults — cracks that have movement on each side — dominate the area, not only as mountain margins but also as an underground plumbing system for hot magmas and mineral-rich deposits.

Men and women followed their dreams and illusions to this area, to found towns like Cochise, Bisbee, Pearce, and Tombstone. They bet their lives and their futures on the lure of metals, wide open spaces, and other less tangible hopes. Because the countryside demands so much, it became a land of eccentricity and rugged individualism.

COCHISE — Kate Crowley

The Cochise Hotel, with its whitewashed exterior and covered boardwalk, looks out on desert shrubs and the distant Dragoon Mountains. Across the road is a railroad track that once kept the Wells Fargo office inside the hotel busy. That was in the days when the junction between the Southern Pacific and Arizona Eastern Railroad lines put the town at the hub of commerce. The mines at Johnson and Pearce and the Green Cattle Company were big business in 1882, when the hotel was built, but today the town is

Faraway Ranch — Chiricahua National Monument. (G. Huey)

sparsely settled, and tumbleweed moves freely down the main street. The railroad days are gone, and the stores are closed, but the Cochise Hotel is still open.

It has a wind-up phonograph, heavy walnut tables and chairs, a tan velvet sofa, and five guest rooms that are simply furnished with a turn-of-the-century flavor. It is a step back into history, at the beginning of a route that is full of ghost towns, abandoned and still active mines, and a variety of historical attractions.

John Rath, a telegraph operator, built the first rustic building that served the community as post office and boarding house. The current owner is Elizabeth Husband, daughter of William Shirley Fulton, the founder of the Amerind Foundation in nearby Texas Canyon. She says, "I always tell people the Foundation is the most important thing, next to the Grand Canyon."

Fulton was a treasure hunter too, but the treasure he sought was the knowledge of the American Indian. He was an amateur anthropologist who worked on surveys and conducted his own scientific investigations of the area. His home was in New England, but his imagination was in Arizona, where he bought the FF Ranch and set in motion the development of today's library, art gallery, museum, and laboratories.

His daughter Liz is quiet and gracious. She would have been described as a fine gentlewoman in the hotel's heyday. She does the bookkeeping and shopping.

But the reason people come to the hotel is really Lillie Harrington, the gruff cook and manager, who is in her eighties and takes no backtalk from anyone. Lillie has been managing the hotel since 1969, when Liz hired her. Lillie was the cook for Liz's parents for many years and was also capable of doing plumbing, electrical, and carpentry work, so it was only natural for Liz to hire her as the manager of the hotel. Lillie's face is deeply tanned and creased from her years in the desert. She wears a plaid flannel shirt over loose fitting pants, and on her bare brown feet are a pair of worn-down flip-flops. She has worked hard all her life and isn't ready to quit.

Lillie describes herself as crotchety and she lives up to the description, yet there is a charm that gives pleasure to those who are not scared off by their first impression. Liz might own the hotel, but she has been unable to put up a "No Smoking" sign in the dining room because of the cigarillo-smoking Miss Lillie.

Miss Lillie and her boss are two older women who have known one another for a long time, and their relationship appears to be more like that of two sisters who have reached old age together.

We found Lillie in the kitchen, taking chicken and steaks out of the freezer and setting them out to thaw for the evening meal.

"Have you got a reservation?"

"Not yet. We just wanted to look around a bit. Is that OK?"

"Well, I s'pose so."

"We plan to be back in December and would like to stay then."

"Well, hell, we don't make reservations that far in advance!"

We assured her we didn't mean to make reservations right away and then we tried to unobtrusively slip into the next room. There are no telephones or TVs in the rooms, and there is no ice or pop machine. In some ways it is like a typical B&B, but the proprietor isn't really interested in running a quaint inn. "Only twelve people can stay here at one time, and I don't encourage people to stay more than one or two nights."

When we return some months later, we call in advance to make reservations for dinner. The menu is presented orally, as Lillie asks over the phone, "Do you want chicken or steak?"

We arrive at the scheduled time of six o'clock (there is only one sitting), and she asks how we want our steaks cooked. Then she directs us to fill out a card, giving vital information, like how we are planning to pay for the meal.

As we eat dinner, we talk with Liz. Lillie shuffles in and out, serving the meal and cleaning up in the kitchen. There is a friendly sort of banter and teasing between the two women, as we ask about the hotel and their lives.

Liz tells us she married a cowboy in 1935 and has been in ranching since then. Then, with an accent that combines Ozark and western twangs, Lillie gives her history. "I moved with my family from Arkansas to Phoenix in September of 1918. I was eleven years old then.

"The first time I saw Phoenix, Central Avenue was paved, where two cars could go on it, as far north as Missoura Avenue, which is not very far north. The rest of the whole country was cotton farms or citrus groves."

Liz cuts in, "I thought you came in a covered wagon," followed by a loud laugh.

"Nooo—We came from Arkansas on a slow train."

When asked how she ended up in this part of the state, Lillie says, "Well, I got married and moved down here and homesteaded. We homesteaded at the foot of the Rincon Mountains and our homestead joined the national forest. We spent twenty years out there."

Then she and Liz spend some minutes discussing and debating over who lived next to them and just exactly where the ranch was located.

Liz says, "I thought you drove cattle."

A low, moaning sigh comes from the kitchen, and with disgust in her voice Miss Lillie says, "Well, somebody might have written that, but I've never found it." Shaking her head, she continues, "One fellow got it down somehow that I used to cook on a chuckwagon.

"My husband and I drove thirty-eight head of horses from the homestead, which was near Pantana, to Young. It was horses we drove, not cattle!"

Liz adds, "That's worse."

Lillie continues, "They're hard the first two days, 'cuz some of them are wild as can be and the others are just old folks, so I was in charge of the pack horses. My father-in-law helped us as far as Tucson. They let the wild ones run for a little bit, right after we let them out, and he helped us until they settled down. By the time we got to Florence, we were having to make all of them go."

"You needed firecrackers," suggests Liz.

There is an obvious affection between the two women, and as the meal comes to an end, it is easy to see that Lillie is not nearly as gruff or intimidating as a first impression would lead one to believe.

When she clears Mike's plate, she says with a touch of surprise in her voice, "My goodness, you ate it up!" As if a person would dare to leave food on the plate!

There are lots of historic places to visit in southeastern Arizona, but very few have the personality of the Cochise Hotel, and if you're interested in an example of the determination and hard shell that developed in the people who were tempered by the desert sun, then the Cochise Hotel and the two strong women who run it are the real thing.

PEARCE — Mike Link

There's not much to recommend Pearce to the traveler. No glitzy signs, no source of refreshment, yet Pearce is attractive; it's a necessary stop in Sulphur Springs Valley. It is an old mining community that began with Johnny Pearce's discovery of silver ore in 1895. (Silver has been the precious metal of the area, more so than gold.) Now the old mine sits on a hillside, looking deserted and forgotten. The history buff can look at the landscape and envision a more industrious time, when riches were taken north to Cochise.

The worn tracks tell about a boom in Pearce that almost emptied Tombstone. The old school is a reminder of a time when more than three thousand people lived here. Historians can see men working hard within the land and the fever of riches.

Of course the miners were not the people who got rich. They were dreamers, looking for their grubstake, laborers trying to survive in a job that denied them sunshine, fresh air, and good health. They worked hard, worked in a suit of sweat, and came out of the mine exhausted and dirty.

The mine sits up on a hill like a temple to the gold and silver gods. It is similar to some of the weathered temples of Mexico—artifacts of humanity's struggle to find their path to glory on earth.

The gravelly streets have a smattering of houses, but the only store that is open is the Pearce General Store, a false-front relic of western development.

Mining machinery decorates the yard. Silent and empty ore cars collect desert sunlight and tourist stares. This is an antique store now, a dealer in time and nostalgia. Most antique stores are surrounded by the present, but the winds that blow from the old mine maintain a sense of past, and the general store has no companions to remind you of the present. The dis-

plays are of interest, the museum has good artifacts, but it feels like they have just been left there and will be put to use again.

Dreams don't die in places like this. Reality says that there will be no skyscrapers here, that the cattle ranches of Willcox can't prosper in the sparse vegetation of the hillside. But the wind whips across the mine opening like air across an empty pop bottle, and the music that it plays keeps hopes stirring. Unlike Courtland and Gleeson, the ghosts of yesterday must share the town with the present.

The Pearce Mine still has ore; it is still owned. One of the owners cooks at the Grapevine Ranch while she and her husband await a grubstake. It is appropriate that the Grapevine should be the place to wait. The tall trees that once grew there are now timbers in the mine shafts.

There are riches below the ground, and dreams above. No one knows if they will ever mix.

SINGING WIND — Mike Link

Winifred Bundy dreams of riches of the mind. Her treasures come bound and printed. North of Benson and the freeway, on Ocotillo Road, is a shot-up mailbox with the words "Singing Wind" written on it. This is the entry marker.

Hang a right on a dirt track that could have served the Butterfield Stage. Open a gate, drive through, and close it again. This is a working ranch, and even if you like books, don't let the cattle out.

Another quarter mile and you come to the ranch house, with its big mesquite door. Cattle, horses, cats, and birds provide the life of the community. The vistas open up on the distant ranges, and a line of cottonwoods marks the San Pedro River.

Winifred may be anywhere on the ranch. Store hours? "If I'm here, fine. If not, tough luck. I detest telephone answering machines. I put the phone by the door and leave the door open and hope I hear, but you never know."

If this sounds like a surefire way to fail at business, remember that this is an eccentric land. She has a book store because she wants one, not because she saw it as a glowing business opportunity.

Win was born in Oak Park, Illinois, to a "General Motors vagabond." By the twelfth grade she was attending her twenty-second school and sixth high school. Her only sense of place was in books, which filled the loneliness of constant disorientation.

She met her husband, Robert, in Minnesota, when he was working on a master's degree, and they married in 1949. He was nine years older than she, but she recalls, "He looked real young." Win had asthma, and the north country had too much humidity for her. Tucson became a goal for them, so when a job opened up in 1952, they didn't hesitate.

To fill her hours, she attended the University of Arizona and earned a bachelor's degree in English and history, and then a master's in history and library science. After her 1956 graduation they bought Singing Wind Ranch.

Win had lots of encouragement from her professors, but none of them saw a connection between her degree and the new ranch. She had a dream of owning a bookstore, but they were too practical to think of a ranch store.

Kids, 4-H, calves, irrigation, holding the roof on when the wind roared through, and other practical matters consumed most of the next seventeen years, but they did not take away the dream.

In an unlikely twist to this quixotic tale, a German shepherd bought Winifred's first stock of books. Robert agreed to board two German shepherds while the owners went to Europe. They barked and chased livestock, and tormented the horses. Finally, one mare could stand no more and kicked one dog, knocking an eye out. Win took care of the dog and gave the owners a $600 bill for feed and veterinary services. That $600 was invested in two shelves of books.

Cars didn't line up in the driveway, and people weren't suddenly watching the ads for a Singing Wind bookstore. What she got was a word-of-mouth advertising campaign, a barbed-wire-service message that brought in "a steady trickle" of customers in pickups and saddles.

She decided to focus on southwestern books to fill her shelves, and eventually two rooms of her home. The shelves, like the big door, are homemade and constructed with mesquite. She collects some out-of-print material, but her prime trade is new publications from small presses. She "won't jack the prices up," and she won't take credit cards. "I'm not going to get involved in that credit card junk." She prefers checks over cash, because she keeps her change wadded up in her pocket.

The book stock keeps growing, and the demand from libraries, locals, collectors, and tourists keeps her busier than ever, which has helped her adjust to the loss of her husband. Now ten thousand volumes keep her scanning and learning. "I try to help the customer. I know most of the books. I scan a lot and I read fast, so I can help most people pick out a book. I think family tradition should include reading together."

A customer might get fresh baked rolls or even an invitation to join Win for a meal. While her fame grows through articles in *Arizona Highways* and *Time* magazine, and through broadcasts on Voice of America and the Canadian Broadcast System, she remains a whirlwind of energy, taking care of the ranch and her customers. Talking to her is like watching a motion machine. She appears to stand still, but her body tenses and vibrates. While she talks, she seems to be looking for a reason to move.

Maybe it's the fact that she was constantly on the move growing up, or maybe it's the wind. "We called the ranch Singing Wind because of the sound of the winds in the mesquite."

Now the sign below the dinnerbell says it all: "Singing Wind Bookshop. Headquarters for books about the Southwest. Please ring bell for service. Stuff of dreams make up books."

TOMBSTONE — Mike Link

"The town too tough to die" is the cliche that Tombstone uses on its promotions, but it is the Old West mystique, rather than the town, that won't go away. The town grew up on silver and gold, miners, gamblers, and gunfighters. Bisbee, twenty-five miles to the south, was probably tougher, dirtier, and more notorious, but it didn't have the individuals who color Tombstone's tales.

John Bourke, captain of the Third Cavalry, wrote in his classic *On the Border with Crook* in 1891: "The completion of the Southern Pacific and the Atchison, Topeka, and Santa Fe systems, and the partial completion of the Atlantic and Pacific Railroad had wrought certain changes in the condition of affairs. . . . In a social sense they had been the means of introducing immigration, some of which was none too good. . . .

"Tombstone, then experiencing a 'boom', had been increased by more than a fair quota of gamblers, roughs, and desperate adventurers of all classes."

After World War II, Americans took a trip back in time and gave the gunslinger, gambler, marshall, and sheriff the masculine virility we associated with the war hero. The 1950s and early 1960s saw a boom in TV westerns, B movies, spaghetti westerns, and Old West memorabilia. We put the Lone Ranger on a white horse, and white hats separated the good guys from the bad. There were no gray areas; we knew right from wrong.

Then the social revolutions of the 1970s reexamined the mythos of the West and the western slipped from the screen, to be replaced by police and doctor dilemmas. But the western hero has not slipped from our fascination. Millions of people weaned on "Gunsmoke," "Have Gun Will Travel," "Wyatt Earp," and "Tombstone Territory" still want to walk the boardwalks of Tombstone. They want to see the famous O.K. Corral, where the feuding families of Earp and Clanton shot it out.

We are fascinated with Sheriff Texas John Slaughter and his Z Brand Ranch, and Ed Schieffelin and his silver mine, "The Lucky Cuss." The gallows at the Tombstone courthouse, now a state park, is a morbid reminder of the wild days, and we temper our disgust with the humor of a coroner's report for a lynched outlaw: "I find that the deceased died of emphysema of the lungs, which might have been caused by strangulation, self-inflicted or otherwise."

Today, the town is more of a Hollywood version of the Old West than the real Tombstone, and we can be glad that it is, because the real item was too tough to enjoy. Bourke describes one episode of the Chiricahua wars that gives us insight into the real quality of the town: "There were other parties in Arizona who disgraced the territory by proposing to murder the Apaches on the San Carlos . . . remembered in the territory as the Tombstone Toughs. . . . They rep-

Tombstone, Arizona. (E. Cooper)

resented the rum-poisoned bummers of the San Pedro Valley, and no community was more earnest in its appeals to them to stay in the field. . . . Never before had Tombstone enjoyed such an era of peace and quiet. . . . All that the 'Tombstone Toughs' did in the way of war was to fire upon one old Indian."

The real story of Tombstone is not Bat Masterson, who went from sheriff to sports reporter, the Earps, Doc Holliday, Buckskin Frank Leslie, Luke Short, Crazy Horse Lil, Lizette the Flying Nymph, nor Irish Mag. They are role players in a bigger drama of flood, earthquake, and depression. Tombstone was a town of bullies, alcoholics, and opportunists, mixed with men and women who were seeking identity and fortune in the last frontier of America.

It was a reckless freedom that existed here if you were fast with guns, knives, and fists. No rules existed unless you could enforce them; that might seem good on the screen, but intimidation and fear were real companions in everyday life.

The hills were denuded to construct the mines, wildlife lost habitat and fell to the gun, and life was just another poker chip. Today the town is an endless row of tourist concessions, and Tombstone is the town too touristy to die.

BISBEE—Mike Link

Eclectic: "Selecting, according to taste or judgment, from different systems or sources. Broad in matters of taste and belief." Substitute "Bisbee," a town and an experience. Perched between the heights of the Mule mountain range and the depths of the Lavender Pit, it is both sparse and opulent.

Mining is both its bane and its glory. Mining brought in a mix of ethnic groups, who divided the town into closed neighborhoods with distrust and violence. "When we grew up here, it was just expected that we'd go to work in the mines." "There was only one really happy day in a miner's life: the day he quit the mines." "When you have kids, you want them to have an education and a job where they don't have to be underground." The mines closed, the kids got educated, and a new breed of Bisbeean moved in.

Homes wind up the one-lane two-way roads to dizzying heights and perch on impossible slopes. The homes represent the slapdash structures of the mining days, with yards outlined in old bed posts or ocotillo fences.

In the monsoon season the streets serve double duty as streambeds, and in winter, snow substitutes walking (or sliding) for driving.

Old Bisbee, the downtown area, Brewery Gulch, and Tombstone Valley combine shops and the history of two "60s"—1960 and 1860. There is an ambience of the "flower child" and hippie, shops without definition except that they are collections of unrelated items. The unifying theme to many shops is the taste of the owner.

While the roadbed is the streambed in Brewery Gulch, there are long linear moats through Tombstone Valley that funnel the river flow into concrete canyons. Homes have concrete driveways that span the moats, often supported by old railroad ties. Even the fire engine must cross a "drawbridge" as it leaves the station.

Accomodations reflect the mining past—the Bisbee Inn, the Oliver House, the Inn at Castle Rock, and the Copper Queen Hotel. Most are old buildings, with mining-period decor, more consistent with the 1860s than the 1960s (except that they no longer put three men in a bed, on eight-hour shifts).

The exception is the Inn at Castle Rock, with rooms titled "Cardinal Sin," "Big Nose Kate," "Sultan's Harem," and "Dirty Shame." It is owned by James Babcock, a recluse, geologist, architect, painter, piano player, and do-it-yourselfer, who professes to have written thirty-six books in one period of his life—a time when he sat at the typewriter and wrote right through on them. The old miners' rooms in this one-time boarding house are gaudily painted, and Jim's paintings—a surf scene beside an old surfboard, a ski scene beside a pair of old skis—are examples of the decor. A verdant garden and the building's design express the owner's eclectic spirit while retaining the old structure.

Perhaps the variety in town reflects the constant rebuilding—the massive floods, the horrendous fires. The Phelps Dodge copper mine was the one consistency, and that no longer operates. The high rollers, the gamblers, the gunfighters, the prostitutes no longer roam Brewery Gulch, and men no longer wear soft hats with long candles into hellish mine tunnels.

Old-timers dreaming of the "good old days" and kids wondering what their "good old days" will be sit on benches outside the Phelps Dodge office, now converted to a historical museum. Tourists step through the doors, eye the displays, touch the equipment, move through the town, and absorb the eclectic energy. Beards and long hair remain the trademark of the entrepreneurs.

The sixties of both centuries were a time of bearded men, of women with strong wills. Both were marked with wars—Civil in one, Vietnam in the other. If history does repeat itself, perhaps Bisbee is even more historic than it advertises. Two generations, not one, are captured here.

Copper mines like the Lavender Pit brought Bisbee glory during their heyday, and depression when they gave out. (L. Parent)

50

THE CHIRICAHUA MOUNTAINS

CHIRICAHUA NATIONAL MONUMENT—
Mike Link

I have wandered in lots of strange places over the years and I have seen arches, canyons, badlands, geysers, mudpots, volcanoes, canyons, and peaks, but no place in the United States compares with the hoodoos of Chiricahua. There is a temptation to think of this as an Indian spirit grounds.

The spirits we find here are the inspirations that we look for in great art. The lines, shadows, and structures are metaphorical. Ignore the hokey names on signs—the impact of this monument is in the different images that it evokes in each individual. Like surrealism and abstraction, this landscape is fascinating and absurd. The rock figures seem to be in motion—rock zombies, flowing down the canyon side. The dilemma is in the reconciliation of this chaotic vision with the orderliness that humans try to impose on life.

Isolated on the western side of the mountain, the monument is just a part of a larger range of mountains, a fragment of the basin and range geography. Geology dominates. The drive to Masai Point exposes lake deposits and tells of a time when the climate was more humid and water was impounded by the volcanic structures.

Sugar Loaf Mountain is a separate volcanic flow, a remnant of what might have covered the hoodoos at one time, but it is primarily another perspective, a higher one for viewing the madcap rockwork. Cochise Head looms behind the erosion, a high dome with a profile that resembles a person. Since Cochise avoided photographs and all the other vestiges of capture and subjugation, we have no idea if this profile resembles the great chief, but its sturdy countenance and quiet dignity and the fact that it belongs here are all reminiscent of the man.

The rocks are rhyolite, a volcanic ash that brewed in the caldera that is now Turkey Creek Canyon. As at Mount Saint Helens, turbulent gases and fine ash poured out of vents and rolled down the main mountain. It was explosive volcanism, with silicic lava that is stiff and resistant to flow, unlike the fiery rivers of Kilauea on Hawaii.

The energy of the event was much greater than at Mount Saint Helens, much greater than humans have ever witnessed in North America. Winds of hurricane force blasted down the slopes, and a plastic flow of magma destroyed all forms of life. It was twenty-five million years ago, but there would have been many life forms in the area.

The eruptions did not happen all at once, but in a series of explosions. Geologists call this a resurgent caldera.

While the flow coursed along the mountainside, ash was thrown into the sky amidst lightning and clouds of gas. The ash cooled in the air and came down to cover the various flows. The hot flow adhered to itself and became welded tuff; the airborne material came down as nonwelded tuff. At first this meant little, but in recent times, after the flow was raised and cracked by uplift and cooling and exposed by erosion of other rock layers, this nonwelded material became part of the sculpturing process.

When the rocks cooled, the material shrank and cracks formed. When the material was uplifted, more cracks developed on the vertical plane. Water seeped in and froze, which meant it expanded and wedged the rock units apart. Running meltwater carved out the spaces between the spires. Then wind began to loosen the unwelded tuff, and horizontal erosion coupled with vertical fragmentation gave us the spirit valley that forms the background and soul of the monument.

It is not just humans that traverse the trails and meander among the forms. Swifts are perhaps the most spectacular birds of the canyon. They dart in rapid flight, their wings held rigid or beating up and down, unlike the violet-green swallows' back-and-forth wingbeats. The white-throated swift darts like a bullet, sweeps down to the stream and takes water on the wing, and then rises suddenly into the sky again. It is

Chiricahua National Monument. (G. Huey)

an aerial bird, even mating in the air.

The swift does not sit on a branch or wire, but it will perch on a cliff side in a communal aggregation of nests that are cemented together with saliva. In this area, it is the white-throated swift that forages for flying insects, like mating ants and swarms of gnats. Because the Chiricahuas do get snow and bad weather, the white-throated swift makes use of its unusual ability to go into torpor—a form of hibernation or suspended animation.

The mammals of the monument are special, too. The Apache fox squirrel is one of the animals that was isolated in the mountain ranges when the climate of the Pleistocene changed the valleys into deserts. This island effect created evolutionary gene pools. The Apache fox squirrel is a native of the Sierra Madre, with an isolated and distinct population in these mountains. There is no other population of this Mexican species in the United States. In the Catalinas, Huachucas, and Santa Ritas are Arizona gray squirrels. Both of these species have been isolated by the natural elimination of lowland forests. Now the Apache fox squirrel exists in the pine/oak woodlands between 5,200 and 7,500 feet.

This is also the northern end of the coatimundi range. A relative of the raccoon, the coatimundi inhabits the Central American rain forests and deciduous zones. In the United States they are stragglers, remnants, and wanderers. They inhabit five of the mountain ranges from about 5,000 to 7,000 feet, in the lower oak/pine forests. There were no records of them in Arizona territory until 1891 in the Huachucas. They may have been extending their range.

They are inquisitive and at times have become campground visitors, but this is to be discouraged. The coati is a climber and will go up both trees and cliffs, but they spend a lot of their time on the ground and often follow javelina trails. The older males are usually solitary, but where they are abundant in the tropics, the females and young males travel in groups of thirty to forty. Here the mountains do not have that many in an entire range.

They are omnivorous mammals, feeding on fruit, nuts, tender vegetation, insects, carrion, roots, and garbage. But we need to understand that, like so many other animals in these mountains, they are living on the edge of extinction, they have very limited ranges, and they are vulnerable to disease (like distemper), feral dogs, development, hunting, changes in the habitat, and snow and freezing, which they don't encounter in the southern part of their range.

CAVE CREEK CANYON—Mike Link

The Chiricahua Mountains reach up to 9,795 feet, and the plant community at that elevation is very similar to what is found along the Canadian border at lower elevations. The rise in elevation from the desert floor is equivalent to traveling north three hundred miles for every one thousand feet of gain. From Portal to the top of Chiricahua Peak is a five thousand-foot

change, the equivalent of fifteen hundred miles (the distance to Prince Edward National Park in northern Saskatchewan).

In Cave Creek Canyon, the creek that runs from the high country brings coolness and supports trees, which provide shade and further coolness. The narrowness of the canyon and the steepness of the rock walls block the sun's rays on each end of the day. As a result, the cooler microclimate of this canyon supports a lush forest at elevations that are normally hot and dry.

This is riparian habitat, the rarest and most important wildlife and plant community in Arizona, and the state's most endangered and threatened. Seventy percent of the state is in federal land, but that has not protected the land, and ninety percent of the riparian zone is damaged.

Arizona sycamore, with its large whitish trunk and flaking brown bark, large maplelike leaves, and seed balls, is the key plant in this zone. It has little wildlife food value, but develops large nesting cavities. Trogons, owls, and coatis are among the animals that benefit from these holes. Without the sycamore, the trogon would not be an Arizona bird.

The forest is narrow, and between the trunks you glimpse the dry agave and yucca growing on the steep slopes. During a 1981 census (when my class counted nineteen trogons), a trogon researcher told us that the combination of canyon wren and hermit thrush meant that we were in trogon country.

Other rare Mexican species live along this valley, including violet-crowned, berylline, and blue-throated hummingbirds, Chiricahua leopard frog, green rat snake, Yacqui black-headed snake, and Sandborn's long-nosed bat (and there are reports of jaguarundi).

The long-nosed bat has a handsome doglike face with an elongated snout. Rather than depend on insects, as most bats do, the long-nosed bat eats fruit and pollen, sticking its long snout down yucca flowers.

Sandborn's is the only long-nosed bat in Arizona, and its pollen-eating habits not only give it a distinctive yellow guano but also make it an extremely important part of the desert ecology. It not only pollinates the yucca and the agave, it also may be an important key to the survival of the cactus. In experiments where a bag was placed over flowers at night, thereby excluding the bats, fewer seeds were produced.

The results of these studies give scientists cause to be concerned that it is the decline of nectar-eating bats that has been responsible for the reduction in cactus and agave reproduction throughout the region. In Mexico, the production of mescal and the bootleg "Bacanora" may be contributing to the bat's decline, since the agaves are harvested heavily in the production of these brews. Such complex ecological webs are difficult to decipher, but common to the natural world.

The canyon is only five miles long, but it goes from

grassland to mesquite and sycamore, to oak and mountain mahogany, then to sycamore, Apache pine, black walnut, and live oak.

Today there are a few people who live in Portal, the entrance to the canyon, and there are people who live up the road toward Rustler Park and the pass over the mountain, but in the canyon it is a collection of bird-watchers, entomologists, lepidopterists, herpetologists, botanists, geologists, and anthropologists. Everyone walks around with binoculars, nets, field guides, taxonomic keys, jars, cameras, and notepads. A plain hiker would look as out of place as an Eskimo in the jungle. This is such a laboratory of speciation, such a collection of rarities, that it might well be classified as a living museum, rather than a wilderness.

Cars don't drive slowly here, they jerk and lurch, the driver leaning out the window, or pressing binoculars against the glass, or calling to pedestrians, "What do you see?" or more likely, "Have you seen the trogons?" At night, campsites aren't lit by campfires; there are bed sheets in the trees and a combination of black and white lights shining on them, while a scientist, amateur or academic, bounces around in khaki shorts looking at what appear to be nondescript little moths clustered on the fabric.

People bring tape recorders, but they don't listen to Bach, the Beatles, or Bananarama; they play owl calls and listen for live singers to respond. There are almost invisible banding nets strung in the trees and the various habitats. Banders wait to pounce on the birds with calipers, scales, and numbered bracelets. The birds not only get caught in a net and must put up with grimy hands and black socks, bags, or containers, but also get their wings, tails, and beaks measured.

Early-morning birders wake up nighttime collectors, who kept up the bird-watchers the night before. Banding nets catch people instead of birds, and one person spooks what another person is watching.

There is a price for all this rarity, which the animals and plants pay. Lizards are caught and marked, sometimes sacrificing toes to scientific curiosity. How would we like a toe clipped off and a big lizard telling us that we don't feel pain? Overzealous observers play tape recorders too much and cause stress when the birds should be concentrating on nesting. Excited bird-watchers trample rare plants, and collectors get greedy.

Wildlife observation requires patience. It also requires ethics. Our observations should never be more important than the survival of the animal.

Above all this activity are shallow caves in the volcanic rock, with shards of pottery and dried husks from two-to-three-inch corncobs. They are a reminder that people have been here for a long time, almost as long as many of the wildlife species. They have survived together by sharing and respecting one another.

Be content to know that the mountain lion might be in the rocks, that the jaguar could someday wander up from Mexico. It is the knowledge that they could be there that imparts the real significance to our stay.

SOUTHWEST RESEARCH STATION— Mike Link

The fact that the American Museum of Natural History maintains a research station here is a testimony to the uniqueness of the area. *Unique* is one of the most overused words in this century of hype, but it is appropriate when it is used in the true sense of its definition: "existing as the sole one, the only example."

The research station began in 1955, when an entomologist went to a friend who was interested in beetles and asked him to buy the land for the museum. The buyer was named David Rockefeller.

The scientist finds five life zones, five very different biotic communities on the side of one mountain range. It is in the transition between two distinct deserts, and combines wildlife from both Mexico and Canada. Every natural science has something to study here, with twenty-five million years of rock records, including 155 fossil fauna, in addition to the 25,000 insect species, 1,370 species of flowering plants, 250 species of birds, 190 lichens, 74 animals, 31 snakes, 24 lizards, 13 frogs and toads, and 4 turtles that live here now.

Human traces date back to 7000 B.C., and history extends through Indians, soldiers, miners, outlaws, and ranchers. Snow covers the mountains and sun bakes the desert. There is a waterfall and a regular flow of water through the canyon. No place on this continent duplicates all of this, and that qualifies as unique. Biogeographers call this area where the deserts and the mountain ranges converge the Cochiso-Hildalgo corridor.

This is the biogeographical junction between the Rocky Mountains and the Sierra Madre. Because of the freezing temperatures of the high country, there are six kinds of pines that grow in the Chiricahuas, and it is the southernmost area of Englemann's spruce and near the limit for ponderosa pine. On the other extreme, it is the northern limit for Chihuahua and Apache pine. The gila monster and desert tortoise reach their eastern extremity, and the Texas horned lizards stop going west.

All of these combinations let scientists explore the intricacies of speciation and diversity. They can observe ranges and limitations. Taxonomists are in their own heaven.

One of the longest projects at the center has been a nineteen-year study of gray-breasted jays (formerly Mexican jays). The study focuses on cooperative breeding helpers.

Originally, people thought that all birds formed couples, bred, laid eggs, and cared for the young, and at fledging everyone would go its own way. But with the gray-breasted jay, they observed a crowd at the nest. They weren't fighting and they weren't eating the young. The questions that needed answering were who are they and what are they doing. Biologists would tell you that each individual maximizes its own genetic future and doesn't care about someone else's.

Fall color in Cave Creek Canyon. (M.J. Hage)

Researcher Jerram Brown observed, investigated, theorized, controlled, color-banded, kept numerous records, observed numerous flocks, and wrote a book, *Helping and Communal Breeding in Birds* (Princeton University Press, 1987), about this type of social interaction. The flock was made up of a breeding pair and their offspring from the last year or two. The young birds helped build the nest, feed the female, and raise the hatchlings. They were waiting for their own time to breed, waiting for an available mate and a good nest site; but in the meantime, they were helping to maintain their genetic future by helping their own parents succeed in raising more young.

Now that this study has been done, people are looking at other bird species, like the bushtit, to see if they exhibit this same behavior. In his book, Brown states that five to eight percent of the birds in the world are cooperative breeders. It is a protective device that encourages mobbing to drive away predators and saves energy by sharing the food-gathering chore. By staying together for a longer period of time, the young birds, like young people, have a longer and better learning experience before starting out on their own.

Another interesting study is the life of the spadefoot toad, an amphibian of the desert, which comes out only when it rains. Their tadpoles have to develop in ponds that dry up quickly. They have one to two days to hatch, and twelve to thirteen to get out of the best ponds. Unlike the jays in Jerram Brown's research, the toads have been studied by a sequence of people, each one picking up a new thread to follow, and a new question to answer.

What tells the toad it is raining? Researcher Mark Dimmitt, who spent many years studying the animals, found that it is the vibration of large raindrops hitting the ground. The toads live underground in a cocoon of shed skin, then emerge with the first hard rain to start calling and mating.

Wade Sherbrooke, research center director, relates the event as told to him: "It tells them that it is now raining hard enough and it is now time to come to the surface and find a pond and breed—tonight! This very night! Your one opportunity during the year! So all these toads respond. The males that find ponds start calling, that attracts more males, and it attracts females, and soon there is a huge chorus of first nighters."

Scientists have found that spadefoot toads have two forms of tadpoles, an omnivorous form, which lives on lots of organic matter from a cowpie or otherwise enriched wet spot, and a carnivorous form, which lives on fairy shrimp and brother and sister tadpoles. This big, robust carnivorous form, with its large head, will grab another tadpole by the tail and chomp its way to the head of its victim.

What is the significance of the two morphs? Each form has the same genetic potential. Why should two survival strategies coexist? What is the switchover that makes an individual a carnivore versus an omnivore? What is the environmental cue?

This study has passed from researcher to researcher, each asking a new and more complex question. For example, one researcher wanted to know how a parasitic flatworm could infest these toads when the flatworm larva is aquatic and the toads are aquatic only one night for eight to ten hours. How do the parasites in the urinary tract "know" when to release their larvae, so that they have the best chance of swimming to a toad, crawling into its nostril, and starting the system all over again?

Research is the base for knowledge. The continual research at the station may provide a basis for solutions to problems of this region. There is concern about the destruction of riparian habitat, the effect of the new smelter across the Mexican border, grazing, the influx of more and more people and industry into Tucson, irrigation, the expansion of starlings into the saguaro nest cavities, the spread of fire ants, the introduction of horehound and tumbleweed, the unnatural increase in mesquite because of cattle and moisture redistribution, and shrub increase where natural grasslands have been damaged.

Economic and ecological sense are not always one and the same, but the growth of understanding and knowledge of our natural world is essential. Wade Sherbrooke summed it up like this: "[Aldo] Leopold said that one of the stupidest questions is 'what good is it?' We do basic research. We ask how the world is put together. Applied research is interested in solving problems of humanity. But to find a solution, they need our basic research to give a picture of how the world works."

THICK-BILLED PARROTS—Mike Link

Dr. Bergtold wrote to the great ornithologist Arthur Cleveland Bent, "It was a great surprise to see how different is a wild parrot from a tame one; one must need get an idea from the latter that a parrot is a slow, lumbering climber, able to use its wings perhaps, yet little given to prolonged and vigorous flight. On the contrary, this thick-billed parrot flew across deep barrancas, from mountain to mountain, as swift and strong on wing as a duck."

Another Bent correspondent, Dr. Wetmore, wrote of a massive invasion of thick-bills to the Chiricahuas in 1917–18. "According to all accounts, Thick-billed Parrots gathered at night to roost in flocks and then spread out in small bands to feed during the day. . . . In Rucker Canyon, the birds came at night to the mountain side above the site of old Camp Rucker.

"As there were a thousand or more here, their morning and evening flights were quite impressive. In the Dragoon Range the parrots roosted somewhere near the head of Cochise Stronghold and made a morning flight that often carried them directly out over the plains to the east. . . . In the Chiricahua Mountains during late fall and winter the birds came down into the foothills to an altitude of between 5000 and 5500 feet."

Thick-billed parrot. (N. Snyder)

Noel Snyder says, "This bird used to be here. Pick up any bird book and it states that up until about fifty years ago, the parrot occasionally came over the border from Mexico to the United States, but it was just a visitor, not a true resident. That was the dogma. There were no nests found in the United States, but then no one was looking for them. Extremely few nests were found in Mexico at that time either.

"Nevertheless, we know from interviews with old-timers that in addition to invasions from Mexico, there were some parrots here all the time, at least in certain areas. People were shooting and eating them. There are actual pictures of wagonloads of shot parrots. They were very vulnerable to shooting because they are noisy, gregarious, and trusting."

Today, Noel and Helen Snyder are attempting to reestablish the parrot population that was eliminated decades ago. They are trying to get Americans to think of parrots as wildlife species, not as escapees from zoos and pet stores.

Noel Snyder worked for the Patuxent Wildlife Research Center, studying the Puerto Rican parrot, Everglades (snail) kite, and California condor, before taking on the challenge of the thick-bill for the Arizona Game and Fish Department and Wildlife Preservation Trust International. Here he works with a very small budget, but as he says, "All the money goes to the parrots." There is no recovery team, no commit-

tee, just a dedication that grew out of a shoestring budget and twenty-nine birds.

The parrot is an internationally endangered species, but not technically a U.S. endangered species, which saves Noel lots of red tape. The bird has no real enemies in the United States, no opposition where laws are needed to aid the project. They are protected by state law, they nest in rotten old snags where logging is unlikely, and they are exciting to Arizonans who get to glimpse the large green bird with a bright yellow strip on its underwing.

This project has no precedent, and therefore no formula. The research efforts change gears constantly; a blueprint could not keep up with the need to react to new situations.

Two flocks, of thirteen and sixteen, were originally released in the Chiricahua Mountains in the fall of 1986. Some birds were lost quite quickly (probably to hawks). Another eight took off toward Mexico and have not been seen since. The remaining fourteen birds stayed through the winter, then took a two-hundred-mile journey north to spend their first Arizona summer on the Mogollon Rim, where Spanish expeditions recorded seeing them centuries ago. Noel believes the Chiricahuas offer better variety of food than they can find up north, but the flock continues to move back and forth between the northern site and the Chiricahuas, establishing their ability to survive and raise young in Arizona.

Conifer forest is needed to support them, and the state has plenty to maintain a large population. The bird grasps a cone in one foot, strips off the scales with its bill, and eats the seeds. Thick-bills eat pine, juniper, and fir seeds, and occasionally acorns and other seeds. In the north, the birds have ponderosa pine and Douglas fir in the highlands, and pinyon pine and juniper at lower elevations. In the Chiricahuas there are a dozen or more conifers. The Chihuahua pine is an especially consistent producer, and its slow-opening cones are available all year. Another parrot favorite is Arizona pine, which is related to the ponderosa and has cones six to nine months a year.

Monitoring the flock presents a real challenge. Without radiotelemetry it would be impossible. Noel would prefer something besides the radio collars he uses, since he thinks they are not entirely harmless to the birds, but there isn't a reliable alternative for monitoring their erratic and long-distance movements.

In the spring of 1988, the main flock had eight birds that went north to central Arizona for their second summer. Prior to this movement Noel released several new radio-tagged birds into the flock. These birds socialized, flocked, and fed with the group, but when the flock flew north, the radio-collared individuals remained in the Chiricahuas. This left only one collared bird in the flock — a female with a radio whose battery was almost dead.

A weak, old radio is better than none, however, and Helen, who handles flying better than Noel (she has a stronger stomach) was soon scouring central Arizona in the Game and Fish tracking plane. Noel followed on the ground. Unfortunately, when the radioed bird was finally located, it was not with the flock. It was all alone and feeding on agave flowers. Two weeks later the bird relocated the flock and her mate, and began to show good mating behavior. Then the radio gave out, and Noel and Helen were not able to keep up with the birds to determine if actual breeding occurred.

In September, the two radioed birds that they had hoped would join the flock in the spring finally flew north and somehow found the main group. The radioed birds had never been in central Arizona, and there were thousands of square miles of pine forest where the other birds could have been. How did the two find the flock? Regardless, Noel and Helen were delighted because the flock was marked again, and they discovered that the flock now contained two fledglings. Clearly, at least one pair bred in Arizona in 1988, and not near the Mexican border, but in the central part of the state.

Then in late October, the flock returned to the Chiricahuas, but the two radioed birds stayed in central Arizona. When I visited with the two researchers in January, they had lost track of the main flock again. Helen had just come back from a long flight all the way to the San Francisco Peaks, but got no signals, so the whereabouts of the two radioed birds were unknown. The Snyders will continue to fly and hope for reports of sightings. Observations by excited individuals have helped them in the past, even though they have had to sort out real sightings from those of both band-tailed pigeons and pinyon jays.

The biggest problem that they face in this effort is a lack of birds to release, despite the fact that as many as one hundred thousand parrots are smuggled across the Mexican border annually. The thick-billed parrot is not involved in the majority of these cases, but it is part of the trade.

The availability of wild-caught thick-bills for release was almost nil between 1986 and 1988. Then thirty-eight birds were confiscated by U.S. Customs in Texas during the summer of 1988. This catch looked promising for the release program, but eight died in USDA quarantine. The quarantine period is designed to detect Newcastle's disease, but these birds had died of something else. The remaining birds were moved to a second quarantine in El Paso, where veterinarian Jim Koschmann agreed to hold them to make sure they did not carry a disease that might be transmitted into the wild.

More died from an AIDS-like parrot-wasting disease, which is latent, long-lived, and fatal. Jim Koschmann himself almost died from psittacosis (parrot fever) contracted from the group. There were only seventeen of the birds left by January 1989. While the survivors have all been treated for psittacosis, current veterinary techniques cannot determine if the living birds carry the wasting disease, so these potential "typhoid Marys" cannot presently be put into the release program. Parrot-wasting disease entered from South America only a few years ago and has now spread to captive parrots of all sorts.

How long must the second quarantine last before the birds can be judged safe to release? Are there places that will take a chance on holding them?

With the virtual absence of confiscated birds to fuel the release program, it has become apparent that the solution is to increase the number of captive-reared birds, a slow and meticulous process that can be helped by zoos and captive-breeders.

Noel does not want to remove birds from the wild population in Mexico for the Arizona release program, because the Mexican population is already stressed, but he would like to see the development of a cooperative U.S.-Mexican thick-bill program for research and conservation. Very little is presently known about the wild population in Mexico. For example, are the released birds in Arizona repeating a migratory habit from Mexico when they move between the Chiricahuas and the central part of the state? When the places they have frequented are plotted, the line runs the same direction as the axis of the Mexican mountain ranges.

One thing is for sure: Even with the first confirmed breeding of thick-bills in Arizona in 1988, the population in the wild is still much too small to be considered

The bright yellow flowers of the agave (century plant) are a food source for thick-billed parrots. (E. Cooper)

fully reestablished. Hundreds of individuals should be released. Twelve is a pitifully small number, even if they do make a spectacular sight in flight.

Noel hopes to establish a resident population in the Chiricahuas, because he believes that it would be better able to withstand natural and cyclical fluctuations in food supply; but so far, all wild-caught released birds have had a strong tendency to migrate. Captive-reared birds might be the source of a resident flock, if the migrations are not innate and if the captive-reared birds don't follow the wild ones that are already making the journey.

However, there are problems with releases of hand-reared birds. An experiment run by Noel and Helen in 1987 showed that even though such birds can be taught to eat cones, they show no aptitude for survival in the wild. Several hand-reared birds that were turned loose would not even flock, which is the parrot's main defense against hawks. Moreover, they refused to eat pinecones once they were free, even when they perched right next to the same kind of cones they had eaten in their cages. Behaviorally they were a disaster, and all were recaptured.

Much better results were had in the release of a parent-reared captive bird. This bird was simply launched into the air in the presence of the wild flock and it quickly joined them, showing behavior identical to that of released wild-caught birds. Thus, birds reared by their parents in captivity show good potential for establishment in the wild, unlike hand-reared individuals.

To complicate the situation, parent-rearing is generally less successful than hand-rearing in captivity, because the pairs usually raise only one chick and ignore the second (in the wild they regularly raise two and sometimes three). To combat this mysterious tendency, Noel and Helen have attached the nest box to the side of the cage, not in it, and feed the second bird while the parent is out. This way the parents are not stressed and the "eyedropper" bird still learns to socialize with other parrots. It has worked so far.

There are lots of surprises in any research. For ex-

60

Winter storms are not uncommon in the Chiricahua Mountains, where peaks reach over 9,000 feet. (N. Snyder)

ample, one pair of birds laid an egg just five days before their scheduled release. The birds were held, more eggs were laid, and the young were successfully raised, but the program had to adjust.

An aviculturalist, who probably had illegal birds, tried his own release on Kitt Peak in 1988. This was poor habitat and the success of his attempt is questionable and unknown. The Snyders would have gladly accepted these birds. In another situation, four thickbills came in with their heads dyed yellow so that they would look like the legal yellow-headed Amazon.

There are lots of places, like the Arizona Sonora Desert Museum, where anonymous doorstep donations could be made, and the birds would reliably end up in the release program. Every bird has the potential for breeding or release, and it is estimated that there are currently more than one thousand in private hands.

Noel describes all released birds as at a disadvantage until they have gained flight strength, a process that takes several weeks. The parrots depend on flocking for defense, but immediately after release they are not capable of flocking consistently with the wild birds, even though they apparently want to — they just can't keep up.

When the new birds are released and squawk, the flock will interact with them for a while, but sooner or later the flock flies off; at that point the lack of conditioning in the caged birds shows up and they lag behind. During this period the majority of their losses (fifty percent) occur, mainly from hawk predation. After the initial exercise period, losses are only about ten percent annually.

The area will survive without the parrot, but it will be more colorful with it. Noel has followed his own migratory route from Philadelphia to Cornell and all the places his various projects have taken him, but the enthusiasm for this program is very apparent. "What motivates us most is the esthetics of the parrots in the wilds," he says. The rest of us can look forward to sharing the beauty.

THE HUACHUCA MOUNTAINS

RAMSEY CANYON—PRESERVING DIVERSITY—Kate Crowley

The road is so narrow and deeply rutted that if you weren't sure of your directions, you'd think you'd taken a wrong turn up a mountain jeep track. It may be an intentional means of discouraging the joy-riding casual tourist from visiting, and that doesn't disappoint the managers of Ramsey Canyon Preserve.

With virtually no advertising, other than word of mouth, they get more than thirty thousand visitors a year. Even though birders are notoriously early risers, the preserve does not open to the public until 8:00 A.M. In order to accommodate so many people in such a restricted area, they require reservations for day visits, and overnight reservations are made months in advance. There is no charge for Nature Conservancy members, but nonmembers are asked to make a voluntary donation when they visit.

The preserve is situated in a narrow gorge on the eastern slope of the Huachuca Mountains. It incorporates 280 acres that are bounded on three sides by the Coronado National Forest. The Nature Conservancy acquired the property in 1974 through a bequest from the estate of Dr. Nelson Bledsoe. In 1975, the Conservancy added Mile Hi—a twenty-acre section of property, including six cabins, that adjoins the Bledsoe property.

Ramsey Canyon is a unique ecological environment. In recognition of this it has been registered by the U.S. Department of Interior as a national natural landmark. The combination of a year-round stream, steep canyon walls, and an east-west orientation has created a moist, cool, and stable environment with five major biotic communities in the canyon: pine-fir, pine-oak, oak woodland, mesquite grassland, and riparian.

The Nature Conservancy was chartered in 1951 as the only nationwide private nonprofit organization that is solely devoted to the acquisition and management of ecologically significant lands.

According to Debbie Collazo, former manager at the Mile Hi, "We get over one thousand new members (to the Conservancy) a year from people who come up here." And though they are not an environmental education group per se, they do believe in instilling ethics and knowledge in their visitors. Debbie says, "One of the ways we educate people is by the basic rules. We're asking them to stay on the trails, so the plants aren't crushed; we ask them not to collect anything, and to leave their dogs in their cars. These are very basic concepts in environmental education."

Her husband Tom, also a former manager, adds, "We do put limits on the number of people who can be in the area. This is a new concept—for a lot of westerners in particular. An area like a canyon that is in a mountain range, which is wilderness, and seems to be part of the great wide open spaces, is actually an extremely finite and fragile resource. The type of limits now in effect in Ramsey are starting to be put in effect in Madera Canyon, on Mount Lemmon, and in Aravaipa Canyon. Our most valuable wildlife areas are real magnets for naturalist travelers, and they are reaching their maximum carrying capacity."

According to Debbie, "People come here to enjoy peace and quiet. It's really filling a need. We're not antivisitor, but we have two main goals: one, to protect this land, and two, to balance that with appropriate visitation." To help maintain this balance, no picnicking or pets are allowed.

We hiked up into the canyon with one of the staff on a warm April morning. We walked along the wooded trail, under branches of big-tooth maple and Arizona oak, past an old abandoned log cabin, through a gate, and parallel to the stream. Overhead in the clear blue sky, a pair of immature golden eagles circled on the rising thermals. Our guide, Don, who described himself as a "maniac from Maine," told us that the birds will practice courtship behavior, leaping off the high rocky cliffs and soaring across to the opposite side.

A stream flows all year long through Ramsey Canyon, attracting wildlife and nourishing a variety of plant communities. (G. Gnesios)

He reported in the newsletter, "I had a great time watching the immature golden eagles (2–3 years old) go through their courtship. This included talon grabbing and tumbling towards earth, only to release each other just in time. I also observed something I had only read about. The bird I believed to be the male passed a stick to the female in the air, which she accepted. This is, I believe, the very beginning of their courtship. If she had not accepted this stick, the male would very likely have to look elsewhere for his mate. I watched them work at building up an abandoned nest on the cliffs just south of the Mile Hi parking lot, only to decide at that point that perhaps they were just a little too young for this. With any luck they will be back next year to raise their young."

Don also told us about some of the wildlife that wanders in and out of the canyon. He stayed in a small house on the property and has on occasion looked out a window and found a black bear staring back at him. One bear got a loaf of bread and ate it on the porch; the bear was still sleeping there the following morning. Another (or possibly the same one) climbed onto the roof of Don's truck one morning and stayed there until it started to rain. It was a big male, estimated to weigh three hundred pounds. Don has also had visits from ringtails, skunks, and rock squirrels, which are fond of the attic and the space under the floor.

There has been an increasing presence of bears in the canyon in the last few years, which may be due to the increased abundance of berries, acorns, and other good bear food since the "wet" years began in 1983.

For the most part, the bears have been very shy and avoided any human contact, even with the temptation of apple trees along the nature trail. But in the fall of 1987, a large male bear, with an ear tag identifying him as #14, began to appear regularly at the apple trees and garbage cans, and even in the parking lot one afternoon. Although it has not threatened any visitors, there is concern about its fearlessness of people. It may become necessary to trap #14 at some time and move it to a more remote location.

This concerns the preserve staff, because the goal is to keep the canyon as wild as possible. It should be as accessible to bears as it is to people, but allowing more people access means greater chance of confrontations with the bears. It is a dilemma.

We moved further up the canyon, and we began to see lots of quick darting movements in the dry oak leaves. These were yarrow spiny lizards. When animals move as fast as these lizards, you wonder how they could fall prey to another animal, but they do. It so happens that the lizards hatch at the same time as the banded rock rattlesnake, which lives in the canyon. The lizards become the main food supply for the snakes.

When we stopped to catch our breath, we watched two of the yarrow spiny lizards on a rock. The pair grappled with one another like two wrestlers. One inflated its blue throat pouch and then grabbed the tail of the other in its mouth. They spun in a circle, but when Mike touched the tail of one with his hand, they quickly separated and went off in different directions.

Continuing, we climbed over salmon-colored ledges and skirted boulders covered with layers of emerald green lichens until we came to a large waterfall. The only other direction was upward. So we climbed to a high ledge, and part of our group decided to keep going into the national forest land and back by a different route. The rest of us sat in the sun for a while, soaking in the warmth and the serenity of the place, like the lizards beside us.

I was happy to see a clear sky overhead, because it was in this very same spot that a hiking group barely escaped a flash flood in June 1983. There were six in the group that had split off. As they looked up at the waterfall they heard thunder, saw some lightning flash, and felt the first raindrops fall. They continued up the streambed, absorbing the peacefulness of the secluded gorge. And then they saw the wall of dark water rushing at them. Their leader shouted, "Run for it!" and without any delay, they all scrambled up the rock walls, grabbing trees to secure themselves.

Beneath them, the stream grew in size and force, with standing waves lifting rocks and logs. They had climbed out on the side opposite the trail back, so they were forced to bushwhack back to Mile Hi, where they were welcomed with hugs and tears.

Flash floods are always a concern in desert regions surrounded by mountains, but it's been especially bad in Ramsey Canyon since the fire on Ramsey Peak in 1983. Six hundred acres of the watershed were burned.

The day of the flash flood, Tom Collazo was in the Bledsoe cabin waiting with the rest of the original hiking group. The cabin is built over the creek, and Tom says, "We heard this huge roar come up and the water came up to the floorboards. The cabin acted as a bridge, so we were able to get the group out on the right side of the creek. The rest of the group finally came down, later in the day, looking pretty bedraggled. We did a pretty good business that day selling sweatshirts, because everyone was soaked."

Every time it rained for weeks after that, "The creek ran black and smelled of humus. Years worth of topsoil were washed away."

We talked to Tom and Debbie in October 1987, the year before the Yellowstone fire, and in a somewhat prophetic vein Tom said, "Smokey the Bear has done such a good job of suppressing fires now, it's created a situation that there are excess buildups. Every time there's a fire, it's a catastrophe, and it burns all the way into the crowns of the trees. So we need to try to put fire back in its proper place in the environment."

During a summer visit to Ramsey Canyon I was fascinated and thrilled by the number and variety of butterflies that we saw. It is a lepidopterist's mecca, as well as a birder's, because of the number of species that can be found there.

Every summer they hold a butterfly count. Approximately twenty-five people come and wander up

Cobwebs hold together this tiny hummingbird nest. A single nest may measure one to two inches across and less than an inch deep. It is hard to comprehend two eggs small enough to fit in that space. (N. Snyder)

and down the canyon surveying the butterfly population. The average year yields anywhere from sixty-five to eighty species. The best count occurred in 1983, when ninety-six species were seen. According to Tom, "The big butterfly counts indicate that this is a very healthy and diverse environment, and it needs to be protected."

I was able to identify only three species on our hike, but they were all beautiful. The most commonly seen was the western tiger swallowtail. One cluster was probing wet spots on the roadway. They moved about on black threadlike legs, with their black and yellow striped bodies between large yellow wings edged in black, with blue highlights.

The Arizona sister is a black-winged butterfly, with orange spots on its wingtips. Chasing one another through the air were a pair of pipe-vine swallowtails. They also have black wings, with a wash of iridescent blue near the base of the wings. The butterflies are as beautiful to behold as the more popular hummingbirds.

But, there is no question that it is the hummingbirds that are the main attraction at Ramsey Canyon. In the six years that the Collazos lived at Mile Hi, Debbie came to the firm belief that "Hummingbirds are *the* most popular family of birds in the world. There are other birds that people like a lot, like puffins and owls, but I'd still say the hummingbirds, overall, are peo-

ple's favorite bird."

One of the first sights that greet the visitor who enters the preserve parking lot is a row of lawn chairs and benches, usually filled with people, lined up three feet away from an assortment of hanging hummingbird feeders. Sometimes there are people standing behind the seated observers, waiting for a space to open. The feeders are hung on branches and on a line that is strung between two trees. Most people hold binoculars in one hand and a field guide in the other, alternately looking up and down. Some people hold cameras and try to catch the little hummers as they pause at a feeder.

In front of the various cabins there are more bird feeders, and here the serious photographer can mount a camera on a tripod and spend an entire day waiting for the right moment to snap the shutter. A project to plant native hummingbird flowers in the feeder area and around the cabins will allow photographer and pure observer alike to see the little birds hovering in front of and sipping the nectar from natural feeders, such as Bouvardia, lemon sage, and betony.

Some people can sit for hours in the hummingbird "peanut gallery," like the older woman we saw wrapped in a serape and perched on a chair when we looked out in the morning, and still there just before noon. Hummingbirds can do that to you, mesmerizing you with their robotic movements.

A violet-crowned hummingbird sits on her nest. (N. Snyder)

What's more difficult to understand are those people who have no time, who only want a reason to make checks on their lifelists. They buzz in and buzz out, just like the birds they've come to see.

Some professional natural history tour companies fall into this category. As Tom explains, "A couple of fifteen-passenger vans zoom up, they all pile out, and the leader calls out all the species they see, and then they hop back in the van and leave. They think they've seen Ramsey Canyon, but they haven't *seen* Ramsey Canyon.

"On the other hand, they don't impact the other parts of the canyon. There's some good reasons to have the hummingbird feeders in the parking lot."

I've added eight species of hummingbirds to my list on my visits to southeastern Arizona, seven of them at Mile Hi. There are fourteen possible species that can be seen at Ramsey Canyon, depending on the season and your luck. At one sitting we watched a rufous at a feeder. It is a pretty bronze-backed bird with a brilliant necklace, as bright as polished gold or copper, but with a bright orange cast.

I had some good looks at the magnificent hummingbirds, too, as they sat at the feeders, leisurely sipping the nectar. They are larger than most other hummers, measuring four and a half to five inches long. They look all-black until they come into the sun and their regal purple caps and turquoise bibs flash.

John James Audubon was right when he described the hummingbird as "a glittering fragment of the rainbow." There are not enough adjectives to adequately describe the shocking brilliance that these little birds display as they gyrate in pools of sunlight. The bright feathers appear black until the bird, the observer, and the sun mix in just the right series of angles. Then an iridescent fire appears as the light dances in the feathers, is scattered, reflected, and absorbed.

The little black-chinned hummers seemed especially aggressive, but that is typical of all hummingbirds, especially during mating season and migration. We met one man, Vern Dorman, who is known as the "hummingbird man of Patagonia" (he has almost as many feeders around his house as they have at Mile Hi), and he told us, "The book says the hummingbirds are pugnacious and I say they like to fight."

When riled up they will challenge and chase birds many times their size. One observer reported seeing a nesting blue-throated female on different occasions chase a jay, an acorn woodpecker, and a hermit warbler. Others have seen them dive bombing cats and squirrels and even chasing hawks.

They argue relentlessly with one another over feeding territories since their metabolism requires them to consume one half their weight in sugar daily. Their energy output is equivalent to ten times that of a person running nine miles an hour. With that sort of energy requirement, a person would have to eat 300 pounds of food and drink 150 gallons of water per day.

One little female Anna's hummingbird sat on the opposite side of the feeder close to us. She would stop eating and stretch her neck up so she could look over the feeder, then her hairlike tongue would squirt out as she dipped her head back down to the feeding hole. As she licked the nectar (approximately thirteen licks per second) capillary action drew it into the tongue.

But the birds do not live on nectar alone. To get extra protein they also eat insects—very small insects, which might be found inside a flower. They may also catch an insect in midair.

An Anna's hummingbird at Mile Hi was once observed picking insects out of a spider's web. This can be a dangerous maneuver for the little birds, because they have been known to get stuck in those same webs and become a meal for the spider.

Most "hummingbird flowers" have long, tubular shapes and provide no place for a bird to perch while it feeds; so the bird hovers, with its wings moving in a figure eight pattern. The wings are attached to the body so that the bird is capable of rotating them 180 degrees. Large, well-developed flight muscles give the wings as much power on the upstroke as on the downstroke. This gives the hummingbird an advantage over other groups of birds; twenty-five wing-beats of a hummingbird would count for fifty for another bird.

Some of the most amazing facts about these birds relate to their frequency of wingbeat. For instance, during courtship flights, the ruby-throated hummingbird beats its wings two hundred times per second!

Hummingbirds' feet are normally tucked up close to their bodies, but they may perch to feed. I watched one hummingbird hover near a hanging feeder. This particular feeder was ceramic and had six feeding holes, but only three had perches below them. The bird apparently expected to find a perch, because as it hovered and fed, its feet pedaled on the ceramic, trying to get a foothold.

If the birds are like jewels, then their nests are the hidden treasure chest. The nest, which is shaped like a cup, may be no more than two inches across, about the size of a golf ball, and is excellently camouflaged with lichen and moss. It is generally built on the fork of two branches and well concealed by overhanging foliage; the nest may be built anywhere from a foot off the ground to forty or fifty feet up in a tree.

For many years a blue-throated hummingbird had a nest under the manager's house at Mile Hi. The house extended out over the stream, and the nest was about six feet above the water. At the junction of two long nailheads, the hummingbird had built a series of superimposed nests that measured a total of five inches in height and two and a half inches in diameter.

Hummingbird nests are entirely composed of cob-webs, all carefully woven into a continuous cylinder. The author of *Arizona and Its Bird Life* saw the nest at the house at Mile Hi and calculated that it contained approximately fifteen thousand miles of spider and insect thread, certainly worthy of a Guinness record.

It is not unusual for hummingbirds to raise two or three broods per season, but since they normally lay two eggs at a time, the sum total of a season's nesting is equal to a single nesting of many larger birds.

It wasn't until 1986 that a formal research project about the hummingbird population dynamics was undertaken at Ramsey Canyon. With the project designed to cover five years, the researchers hope to answer some of the questions visitors and staff have about the hummingbirds. For instance: About how many hummingbirds are in Ramsey Canyon in July? Are there as many today as there were five years ago? Do the same hummingbirds return to Ramsey Canyon each year?

Two medical doctors, David Ferry, a cardiologist and experienced bird bander, and his wife, Linda, proposed the study, got it approved, and began with three banding sessions in 1986. They banded during spring and fall migration, and in midsummer to study the breeding population.

The captured birds were banded with featherweight aluminum bands, and measurements of wing, tail, and bill were taken, as well as data on species, breeding status, age, and sex.

The first year, 444 hummingbirds were banded. Black-chinneds were the most abundant, with forty-five percent of the total; followed by Anna's at twenty- six percent, and then the large humming-birds, the magnificents and blue-throated. The first violet-crowned hummingbird ever banded in the United States was found that year also.

The second year of the study they banded 328 hummingbirds of eleven different species. They also banded birds forty miles away at Madera Canyon. One striking difference that was discovered was that 267 broad-billed hummingbirds were banded at Madera and only one at Ramsey — a recapture of a male banded the previous year.

About thirty percent of the 340 birds banded the first year were recaptured the second year. There were twenty-five more young Anna's hummingbirds in the second year. Before 1971, this hummingbird was rarely found in Arizona in the summer. The study may show that the Anna's is becoming a rival of the black-chinned, currently the most common nesting hummingbird in the canyon. There is some fear that the more aggressive Anna's may drive other species out.

The population of hummers may change in composition, but it is certain that there will be no drop in the interest they instill in people. Lush Ramsey Canyon will continue to act like a magnet for birds and birders alike.

RARE AND ENDANGERED PLANTS—
Mike Link

What makes a plant rare? Sometimes it is the ravages of development, a culprit that appears too frequently in this text. Sometimes it is the result of evolution—a species is dying because of its limited ability to adapt to climatic pressures and changes. It may be that we are looking for it at the end of its range, in an isolated refugium where populations are mere remnants of an older age when the climate was different and the plant communities had a different composition. A species may be endangered because its pollinator or planter has been destroyed, or because new competition has been introduced from other continents. It may also be rare because it is in an isolated location where genetic drift has created a new species from a much more common ancestor.

The mountain islands may combine all of these factors in their botanical oddities. Where I live, people fight alien thistles, dig and tear out Russian, Scotch, Canadian, and other introduced species. We tear our hands on the spines that protect the plant and we try to keep it from crowding out the native plants. But here in the Huachucas is a huge thistle that totally lacks spines. It is a native thistle that feeds the abundant hummingbirds, but has not needed the protection of spines, except where we have introduced our domestic grazers. Spineless thistle in the land of cactus!

It doesn't take long to discover that Arizona is either special or extremely provincial. There are the Arizona sycamore, the Arizona cypress, Arizona walnut, Arizona rosewood, and Arizona white oak. There is also the Huachuca agave, which is limited to the area around one mountain range. It has a similar ecology to the other agave, depending on hummingbirds, bats, and nectar-eating insects for pollination, but this isolated species has a different leaf and slightly different flower than its relatives.

There is a long list of special plants, most of them in small and sheltered habitats, in these mountains. For example, in 1980, the tepic flame flower was found in the Huachucas on flat, barren rocks, with small pockets of soil in natural depressions. The soil could be eroded by a cloudburst, or unearthed by Vibram hiking shoes. The plant is less than two inches tall (the whole plant, not the flower), with succulent leaves that rise in a loose rosette on reddish petioles. The flowers are bright yellow and five-pointed, at the ends of slender stalks. There are fewer than fifteen locations in the United States and Mexico where these are known to grow.

Lemon lilies are much larger, with flowers three to four inches across. They are yellow, with reddish brown spots in the throat of the trumpetlike flowers. The leaves grow in whorls on the slender stem. The whorls are widely spaced along the five-foot height of the plant. Compared to the flame flower, these large plants seem like they should withstand anything, but they are known only in California and the Huachuca Mountains. In this range they have been ravaged by fire, and they were eliminated in Carr Canyon after a flood followed a fire. Even where these threats have not been present, one population was found to have an insect infestation that was weakening the plants so that they broke in the breeze.

Endangered plants can't move, they can't be transplanted to suitable habitat, they can't migrate, and they can't reproduce without pollinators. Rare plants need the kind of special concern the Nature Conservancy gives them—inventory, observation, and protection. We talk about the possible cures to horrible diseases that we might lose when we lose a species, the benefits to humans that disappear before they are ever discovered, but the real purpose for saving a species is really much simpler than that. We should save it because it belongs, because the earth is richest when all of its varieties exist, and every species has the right to survive.

Pipevine swallowtail butterfly. (J. Honcoop)

THE SANTA RITA MOUNTAINS

MADERA CANYON—Mike Link

The Indians knew that certain lands were sacred, and they were not afraid to say so. Sacred places were part of the Indian/earth relationship. In our modern culture, we designate scientific and natural areas, but not sacred and spiritual areas. We don't even talk about them.

That does not mean they don't exist, it just means we don't admit it. If there wasn't a special significance to Mount Wrightson, would hiking groups from Green Valley and Tucson join strangers from around the world in a five-mile trek up narrow, winding trails to scale its summit? Would people regularly make the pilgrimage to the summit in the heat?

Mount Wrightson is the parent to Madera Canyon. It is the kingpin to the Santa Rita range, an agglomeration of volcanic and sedimentary rocks. Here thrust faults put Paleozoic sediments against a Precambrian core, and a step may span a billion years.

The summit looks over the land of the missionary, Fort Huachuca, the borderland of Mexico, Tucson, and the valleys and mountains that blend into blue haze, but the dominant sight is Madera Canyon as it slices the mountainside and spills out into a massive alluvial fan and experimental rangeland.

On the saddle are red-faced warblers; in the canyon, hummingbirds of all descriptions, hepatic tanagers, Williamson's sapsuckers, and other delights that read like a menu for a birdwatcher's dream.

The canyon is narrow, flowing down from pine/oak and yucca/manzanita slopes to a sycamore streambed. Water gurgles over rock slabs, cools and soothes the landscape. As in the other canyons of this region, it is the sycamore and the vegetation of the riparian zone that support the greatest diversity of animal life.

The Forest Service looked at Madera Canyon as a picnic area, a multiple-use access to Coronado National Forest, but others spoke for the birds, the plants, the lizard, and the land. Mount Wrightson was given wilderness designation, and Dave and Lyle Collister were told that they would not have to leave the canyon and their Santa Rita Lodge. Instead, they were given a twenty-year lease and told to serve the naturalists. They already were doing so.

Dave, a Californian who roamed Mexico and Arizona, fell in love with Madera Canyon. He worked in Tucson and had a resort and restaurant in the grasslands, but the opportunity to own a resort in Madera Canyon was an option he could not turn down. Even when his restaurant burned down, he kept his enthusiasm for the area.

He even thinks of the loss of the restaurant as a positive experience, because it lessened the impact and visitor numbers in the canyon. Now he tries to share that philosophy with the Forest Service.

When they wanted more people and more picnic tables, he tried to share his perspective: "What about the refuse, how about the trampling and nest disturbance in the riparian zone?"

Madera continues to be a birder's paradise. In a 1986 bird-banding project, 675 hummingbirds were banded in Madera, compared to 444 in Ramsey Canyon. Numbers in Madera Canyon rose to 881 in 1987, then dropped to 668 in 1988, when the flowers were so abundant that the hummers dispersed throughout the mountains. Two blue-throated fledglings traveled from Ramsey Canyon to Madera, and a berylline went back and forth four times in one summer. The Anna's hummingbirds have not been taking over here, as they seem to be doing in Ramsey.

I have found numerous trogons in the Cave Creek area, and I have worked to find trogons in the Huachucas, but until my last trip to Madera, I had not found them in the Santa Ritas. It was a hot day and it was more comfortable to be in the mountains than to be in Tucson. Kate and I moved slowly up the valley and stopped at the picnic grounds, one of the first birding stops.

There were a few different birds here, but the one

The stream that runs down Madera Canyon creates a rare and valuable riparian habitat. (D. Dietrich) that entertained us was the clownlike acorn wood-pecker, a gregarious, noisy bird.

I tend to think of acorn woodpeckers and alligator junipers together, primarily because that is where I first met the bird. I was in a campground, trying to see everything that moved, and a woodpecker flew to the tree. The woodpecker came in ten feet up and on the backside, then it dropped down to eye level and worked its way around the trunk. At the point where I could first see the bird, a shaft of sunlight penetrated the canopy and acted like a spotlight. In *The Birds of Arizona*, Phillips, Marshall, and Monson describe the acorn woodpecker this way: "This white-eyed clown . . . has a harlequin face." That's what greet-ed me.

An intent birder is a serious observer. There is ten-sion in the binocular hunt, and there is a sense of emo-tional warmth when a new species is discovered, but it is the acorn that provides the most amusement for me.

There is more to these woodpeckers than noise and motion. They do more than raid hummingbird feed-ers. They are successful and they are common, because they have adapted a lot of good survival strategies. They are communal nesters; they are social feeders like the gray-breasted jays; they fly-catch like king-birds, only with longer foraging flights (this is partic-ularly true after a rain); they store acorns in the bark of dead pines, sometimes placing the nuts individually in little holes. They need oaks, old snags for roosts, and soft wood for storage.

We drove up the canyon to Santa Rita Lodge to look at the bird feeders next, and were startled by a flash of green. Hummingbirds are known for their metallic feathers. They flash lots of reds, and some species fea-ture blue and purple, but this bird was a brilliant burst of green. Not the green of the females or the green-black color of males, but a green that sparkled—a berylline hummingbird, one of the Mexican species that moves into the States periodically.

Each good bird sighting seems to indicate there will be another. A good birding day almost always con-tinues to be good. This makes sense if you consider that there are good bird conditions and there are bad bird conditions; therefore, if the conditions are right for one bird, they will probably be right for many spe-cies.

With that in mind, we drove to the creek at the end of the road, and I left Kate to read and sleep while I walked. I like the feeling of rock hopping, wandering a dry creek bed, exploring little niches, drifting where my interests carry me. All along I was scolded, "*no trespassing, no trespassing*," but I was boisterous myself and the little house wrens weren't about to drive me from their shoreline homesteads. Later, a black-headed grosbeak sang to me.

The stream was choked with rocks, the bed nar-rowed, and the forest closed in. It would have been a good place to stop, but another sound moved down the canyon, a sound without distinct direction, an

echo call—"*co-ah*," repeated over and over. Not musi-cal, but incessant. The call was familiar—in Mexico they call the bird the coa, and here we call it the trogon.

I will never turn back from a trogon's call; there is no bird down here that is more tropical, more exotic. The trogon is a jay-sized bird that sits upright on a branch with its long tail hanging directly below it. It has a bright red breast and a glossy dark back, with a white collar that separates the head and chest.

As impressive as it appears when you spot it, the bird is difficult to find because it is retiring, and will sit very still for long periods.

I moved quickly, but tried to be careful too. Then I met two other men also stalking the trogon. "There it is," we said simultaneously, me pointing behind them, them pointing behind me. We had each passed one bird, but together we were rewarded.

Trogons nest in sycamores, and use natural cavities as roost sites too. Their food consists of fruit and large

The Santa Rita Mountains drop down to scrub-covered foothills and golden grasslands. (D. Dietrich)

insects. The insects are often fed to the young, perhaps as an extra dose of protein.

We observed the birds until their beauty was fixed in our minds and then we left them alone. It was a great day for birding.

LEAPIN' LIZARDS — Kate Crowley

I have always been fascinated by lizards, but as a northerner, I've had minimal exposure to them. These cold-blooded animals increase in numbers as one travels southward into regions where the climate is more suitable for their year-round existence.

Understanding the meaning of *cold-blooded* can help us understand the reptile behaviors we observe when in their element. When we talk about cold-blooded animals we are referring to the means used to maintain body temperature. A cold-blooded creature must rely on external sources to regulate its internal thermostat. Another word that describes this characteristic is *ectotherm*. We humans are endothermic — *endo* means

"within" — and like the rest of the mammals, we are described as warm-blooded because our body temperature is maintained by internal means.

In many ways lizards look like their kin, the snakes, but the addition of four legs makes them less foreign and frightening. We can immediately understand their means of locomotion, and for the most part they are small and nonvenomous. They remind us of shrunken versions of the giant dinosaurs. Hollywood has recognized this similarity and taken advantage of it. More than one lizard has been projected onto the big screen in truly larger than life proportions, to wreak havoc on the puny little humans. Maybe it is the reversal of roles that makes us feel less threatened by real live lizards.

Also in their favor is their nonaggressive attitude towards humans; in fact, one must be extremely quick to catch the majority of lizards. Often it is just out of the corner of the eye that you see them scurrying away. On our various hikes in the Huachucha, Rin-

Elegant trogon. (R. Fisher)

con, Chiricahua, and Santa Rita mountains, they have been the most frequent and entertaining wildlife that we've seen.

On woody, rocky trails, we watch our step carefully and so our eyes catch movement both ahead and beside us. Sometimes we hear a rustling in the leaves, and when we investigate, a small, dark streak shoots out and disappears into a nearby crevice.

That is one of the more frustrating aspects of lizard watching. For the "lister," the person who likes to know the name for each living thing, lizards are a formidable challenge. While they don't really leap, when frightened most can move faster (for short distances) than the eye can follow. The best chance to view a lizard in repose is in early morning or late afternoon, when the angle of the sun is low and the lizard is in the process of "recharging its batteries"—slowly warming up through the solar energy.

Exposed rocks are popular sunning spots. However, even a stationary lizard may be hard to identify. The Peterson field guide *Western Reptiles and Amphibians* has some very nice color illustrations of various lizards, but the majority of species are described only by text and location maps. So as you hold your breath, trying to notice all the minute details on the somnolent lizard, you must flip back and forth from the front of the book to the back, trying to pinpoint the proper species for the area you're visiting. To add to the

problem, sometimes a lizard's best markings are located on the belly, and unless it cooperates and raises itself up, it's unlikely you'll see these features.

Mike and I got lucky on one hike in Madera Canyon. We were on our way down from Josephine Saddle when in a patch of sunlight I caught sight of a lizard poised on a rock. This one behaved differently than others we'd seen. It was a male yarrow spiny lizard, with a beautiful sky-blue color on the sides of its belly and on its throat patch. Apparently it considered me an interloper into its territory, rather than a predator to run from. To let me know I was intruding it rapidly bobbed its head up and down. When that didn't work, it raised itself up and proceeded to do some quick "push-ups," which let me see all the better the beautiful coloration of its scales.

Unfortunately, I didn't respond like another male spiny yarrow and turn away to avoid further conflict. Instead, I stepped a little closer to get a better look, and he immediately turned and slipped behind the boulder. Further attempts to find him were futile, for he simply moved to the opposite side from the one that I was on.

This highly visible form of territory defense has its risks. On the one hand, standing guard and maintaining his territory gives the male a better chance of attracting mates and reproducing, but on the other hand the physical movements and colorful display may at-

74

Blue-throated hummingbird. (H. Snyder)

tract the attention of a more dangerous predator than myself.

The pleasure derived from the lizards seen on our hikes is in the animation they lend to the environment, as well as the diversity. Without doubt they are integral pieces in the puzzle that is the natural world.

While the majority of lizards are fast and adept at evasion, my favorite is a slow-moving, antediluvian-looking creature, who has fascinated people from the earliest times. It is the horned lizard, sometimes called "horny toad" because of a shape and skin somewhat reminiscent of the toad's. Its scientific name, *Phrynosoma*, means "toad-bodied."

Even with its spiny covering, there is something charming about this little reptile. I suspect part of this is due to the unreptilian-shaped head. Compared to the other lizards and snakes, the horned lizard has a much broader, rounded skull, giving it a pug-nosed appearance.

On our journeys to the Arizona desert, they have been a highlight. My son, Jon, has grown up with an even greater fascination for reptiles and amphibians than I, and trips to the Southwest give him an opportunity to explore and make discoveries impossible in our home state. Twice he has found horned lizards.

Finding one in the first place is a difficult task. The scales and spines are patterned and colored in a mix of neutral earth tones that perfectly match the coarse sandy ground it travels over. On top of that, its round body mimics the stones that cover the ground. For protection, it may partially bury itself, with only its head exposed, or flatten its body, eliminating any shadow. The spiny fringe along its sides aids in this camouflage technique. To make this all work, the horned lizard must remain perfectly still. Any movement will automatically be noticed by a hungry predator.

Once the lizard is sighted and put to flight, its chances of survival greatly decrease. There is very little it can do to protect itself. It may inhale and inflate its body to look larger and more threatening, or it might hiss and shake its tail, which if on dry leaves can create a sound similar to a rattler's warning. If approached from behind, it will turn to face the predator. Its most unusual, and probably effective, means of defense, though, is the ability to squirt thin jets of blood from its eyes.

Wade Sherbrooke, a researcher who has studied the horned lizard extensively, wrote, "The second pair of vein-constricting muscles, located closer to the eyes, can, when constricted, completely block the return of venous blood from the region of the eyes and force the blood pressure here to still higher levels. Under this pressure, blood breaks through the walls of the blood sinuses located in the eye sockets. It then flows into the membranes of the eyelids and sprays forth from

A yarrow spiny lizard with a meal in its mouth. (H. Snyder)

the pore of a gland on the edge of each lower eyelid."

This fluid is apparently distasteful, based on observations of dog, foxes, and coyotes that have been hit in the mouth and nose with it. They were seen to shake their heads, and salivate excessively.

It is not surprising that such an incredible behavior would lend itself to myth making among groups of people who share the land with the horned lizard. In Mexico, some people consider them to be sacred toads. They believe that when the reptiles cry, they shed tears of blood.

The ancient people of Arizona, the Hohokam, Anasazi, and Mogollon, incorporated horned lizard designs into their pottery and painting—a practice carried on today by their descendants. The lore and legend of the native wildlife has also been preserved by the Indians. In their view of the world, horned lizards are seen as ancient and powerful creatures demanding respect.

Among Piman Indians, the horned lizards are believed capable of causing sickness and restoring health. If one offends a horned lizard spirit by killing or injuring one or even unknowingly walking on its tracks, sickness will follow that person. A shaman must be called in to sing horned lizard songs, appealing to the animal's dignity and acknowledging its difference from people. A horned lizard fetish may be used in the healing process, as well. Only by appealing to the horned lizard's "strength" and showing it respect is the person cured.

I hope that our encounters with the horned lizards have been respectful. We have picked them up and shared them with others nearby. We have never been bitten, although that does not mean they will not bite, but they do behave quite docilely when held and stroked gently on the head or belly.

Horned lizard. (L. Stone)

On one occasion, we were eating dinner at a chuck-wagon cookout. It had gotten dark and Jon was shuffling in the leaves at the base of a big old cottonwood. He came back holding a four-inch regal horned lizard (identified by the number and formation of horns at the back of its head). At this dude ranch cookout there was a contingent of Italian tourists. They did not speak any English, so I approached their interpreter and asked her what it would be called in Italian. She said there was no translation, so we held it in our hand and the Italians gathered around, talking excitedly to one another. Some stretched out a finger, to touch it, others were content just to look. The video cameras they carried were set into motion.

I slowly enunciated "HORNED LIZARD" several times, pointing to it at the same time. They just shook their heads. After everyone's curiosity was satisfied, Jon took the little celebrity and replaced him in his night nest. I felt that even if the Italians didn't know what it was called, they had seen more of the desert than the saguaros and barrel cactus.

The next morning, though, on an early morning horseback ride, I was in front of two of the Europeans. We had stopped, and on the left side of the trail a little horned lizard went skittering over the rocks. They caught sight of it, and in their rapid exchange I was sure I heard them say, "Horn leezer."

Horned lizards are protected by state laws today, to protect them from the pet and souvenir trade that they suffered under in the past. But their greatest threat will continue to be the expansion of the cities and recreating humans, who destroy or alter habitat that the little "horny toads" call home.

PATAGONIA SANCTUARY

BY KATE CROWLEY

When you visit Patagonia-Sonoita Creek Sanctuary, you might be met by Robin, the official, or Oscar, the unofficial, greeter. Robin is not an avian, though his name was probably the result of some cosmic predestination. Robin Baxter is the preserve manager, and I will let him introduce Oscar.

"He's a spotted skunk that hangs out by Gate 2. We named him that because he likes to climb into the garbage can near the gate."

Every morning when the can is half full, Robin has to come out and pick up the garbage that Oscar has thrown onto the ground. Even when it's empty, Oscar crawls into the can, and then Robin has to come out in the morning and tip the can to let Oscar out. Oscar then quickly scurries up the Mexican elder tree behind the can, where he can observe Robin at work.

There has only been one time when Oscar really was a grouch. As Robin explains, "One day I had emptied the can, and I walked in the next day without even glancing in it. I went down in the preserve and everybody that I saw (like ten people) would say, 'There's a skunk in the trash can at Gate 2, and I tipped it over so he'd get out,' and then the next person would say, 'There's a skunk in the trash can at Gate 2, so I lifted it up so you could get him out,' and then the next person would say, 'I turned it over so he could get out,' and the next person would say, 'I lifted it up so you could get him out.' I think every other person had lifted it up or put it down, one or the other, so the poor thing got tossed so much, by that time he was really pissed." Needless to say, Oscar responded in angry skunk fashion when Robin came to the rescue.

Oscar is just one of the many animals that make their home on the 312-acre sanctuary. Visitors might see bobcat, coatimundi, javelina, badger, and coyote. Squirrel and white-tailed deer are the most easily seen mammals on the sanctuary. When we first hiked the trails, late in the afternoon, we caught glimpses of several deer bounding through the field and heard the crunch of dry leaves as they made their way through the stand of big cottonwoods by the creek.

But it's not mammals that are the real draw at Patagonia, it's the birds. People come from all over the world to this rare riparian woodland, to look for birds that are found only in this limited range. Over 250 species have been seen here.

We asked Robin what was the major attraction for birders at Patagonia and he said, "The gray hawk. It's probably *the* one they come here for. There's also the rose-throated becard, although it's not right here, but down at the rest area. That's another big one. The northern beardless tyrannulet. It's itty-bitty. It's the dullest, boringest little bird in the world. They come from far and wide to look for this thing. Again, anything with these really limited ranges."

Robin knows how significant the sanctuary is to birders of the world. "I get letters from Europe that say, 'When does this bird come here, cause I'm planning my entire trip to the U.S. around seeing this bird.'

"They spend tens of thousands of dollars every year, just traveling around to bird."

The first bird we saw on our visit was the striking vermilion flycatcher. Earlier, we'd met some women at the popular roadside rest area, and they mentioned they'd seen the flycatcher at the sanctuary. As we drove up to Gate 4, we saw a flash of red and black flying past. Mike got out of the car to look, but it flew on.

After walking into the sanctuary, past the creek, and out into a clearing, all of a sudden we saw that flash of brilliant red, and there were a pair of vermilion flycatchers. A kestrel perched on a nearby snag, observing the flycatchers as they flew up and out and back to their perch to eat the insects they'd snatched from the air.

The ruby-red feathers of the male were backlit and glowing in the setting sun. The female resembled the more somber earth-toned flycatchers. In better light, using binoculars, we would have seen a pinkish tinge

Patagonia-Sonoita Creek Sanctuary. (D. Dietrich)

White-tailed deer are commonly seen in the sanctuary. (G. Huey)

to the feathers on her flanks, but the light was fading and it was quickly becoming too faint to bird by, so we walked out on a trail that took us to Gate 3.

We hadn't walked far down the road when we heard a rattling, scattering sound behind us and turned to see an old pickup, surrounded by a cloud of dust, coming our way. It stopped when it got even with us, and we met Robin Baxter. He obviously enjoys his job and the chance to meet people who come to the sanctuary. He asked what we'd seen and where we were from, and answered questions we had. He gave no sense of being rushed, and volunteered to be of service, if need be, on future visits.

Six months later, on our return visit to the sanctuary, he met with us to share his knowledge of and insights into Patagonia-Sonoita Creek Sanctuary. He dressed casually, wearing khaki shorts, a Nature Conservancy T-shirt, baseball cap, and jogging shoes. We noticed a slight limp when he walked and then saw that his left leg below the knee is artificial. In a roundabout way, Robin's loss of leg and foot led to his involvement as a birder and employee of the Nature Conservancy.

He explained, "It's a great story. It's a wonderful story. I was going to school at Sonoma State. In fact it was my first semester and I was on semester break, which was in January. I was going to spend a week in Yosemite and then go down and spend a week in Death Valley.

"I went up to Yosemite and was just day hiking. I had a campsite down in the valley and was going up to the Vernal/Nevada Falls. I just had on cowboy boots and jeans and a day pack with lunch in it. I wasn't out for heavy hiking or anything, but I took this one path between Vernal and Nevada Falls. There's one piece of trail between the two falls that traverses a cliff face. It's just cut right across the cliff. I walked out on it and it was the middle of January, there was snow everywhere and everything was frozen and icy. I slipped and fell off the cliff, about fifty feet in free-fall, and dislocated this left ankle when I landed.

"I noticed my foot was tweaked around. I didn't try taking off my boot until the next day, and by then it was frozen like a roast out of the freezer. It was like a rock and I figured what's the point. I didn't know it at the time, but I also crushed four vertebrae in my back and broke about a half dozen ribs.

"It happened late on an afternoon, and I couldn't walk out, so I spent the night, huddled under my poncho. When you walk by the falls there's a lot of spray, so I brought my poncho to keep from getting wet.

"It started snowing that night. Because of the storm that came in, nobody came out the next day either. I ended up sitting out there for eight days, under this bush. It snowed I think for seven of those days. It

People come to the sanctuary from around the world to get a glimpse of the gray hawk. (N. Snyder)

cleared up for one afternoon and then it started again. Nobody was looking for me, nobody knew I'd gone up there.

"I was nibbling away, day by day on this one little carrot, and this whole week I'd been just eating snow for moisture. I had four dates every other day. I had enough dates to last till June. I was going to be there when some kid came up in bermuda shorts, as far as I knew, to find me in the spring. I was going to last, I wasn't going to run out of food or anything.

"The day I got found was a clear, beautiful day and I'd been calling all day for help. I'd call and wait a few minutes and I'd call. It got to be late afternoon, just about the same time I'd fallen, about 4:30 or so in the afternoon. I'd quit calling, I figured at least the weather's nice, you know one more day someone will come out here. Somebody's got to come out here! This is getting boring!

"As I was laying there, without hearing anything else, a Stellar's jay, the jay of the pine forest, came and landed overhead and started squawking and I thought there was something real odd about that, and then it dawned on me that that was the first living thing I'd seen in eight days. I hadn't seen a squirrel or a spider or a deer. Nothing. And then this thing landed overhead and started squawking at me, and I clicked on it, and I realized that jays often move up canyon of people and squawk a warning ahead of them. I must have

looked like a bear or something under that bush by then, and he just figured, 'Well, I better let this critter know somebody's coming here.' And he landed over me and started squawking and I made that connection. I thought, I'll just call out one more time, and I called, 'Help,' and somebody answered me and then the bird flew off."

With a chuckle he added, "I always say that birds saved my life, so I turned into a bird-watcher."

And how did it get him his job? "I had already had this interest in natural history. In my last semester of school, I needed a job, these things aren't cheap," he taps his left foot, "and the counselor asked what I liked to do. I said I liked to watch birds. So I got a job at the Audubon Preserve at Richardson Bay. I was their very first intern."

It's easy to talk to Robin and to believe him when he says that he's a people-oriented person, that he likes dealing with the majority of the people who come to the sanctuary.

It's also easy to understand his frustration in managing the property when people consider themselves outside the bounds of the rules. "Bird-watchers sometimes think they do no harm. That rules don't apply because 'I'm a bird-watcher. I don't have to stay on the trail, because I'm a bird-watcher.' 'I can camp overnight in the parking lot, so I can get up early, 'cuz I'm a bird-watcher.' The problem with nature pho-

Northern beardless tyrannulet. (D. Collister)

tographers is the same. 'I can go wherever I want 'cuz I'm only taking a picture.' Artists too. 'We're only painting.' Everybody has a personal, logical reason why they shouldn't adhere to the regulations."

He parodies, " 'How am I supposed to see the gray hawk that I came all the way from Detroit to see if I don't get to go where I want to go?' " and suggests, "Try again another day, if you don't see it today."

While we talk to Robin, we sit on an old bridge abutment where a train used to cross the creek. The stream trickles and twists below us. It is a very lush setting, with huge Fremont cottonwoods lining both sides of the creek. Riparian areas are conspicuous, because compared to the surrounding areas, they have thicker, denser vegetation. The trees that dominate a riparian habitat are the Fremont cottonwoods, willows, Arizona sycamore, velvet ash, and walnut. On the ground there is usually a lot of debris—old leaf material and fallen timber. They are also noisier places, because they contain more life.

It is October and the hottest months are past, but this deeply shaded woods and waterway are peaceful and refreshing at any season. Cottonwood stands and streams like the Sonoita were once more common in southern Arizona, but pressure from farms, communities, and grazing stock have greatly diminished this type of deciduous habitat. Patagonia Sanctuary is probably the very best remaining example in the state.

In the dappled light of midafternoon, two red skipper butterflies, deep rusty-orange in color, skim over the creek, then four fly by us, two in a coupled pair. A black phoebe lands on a nearby branch, and another bright red bird, a cardinal, flys to a perch and begins a staccato stream of "*chip-chip-chip.*"

The other sound that flows up and down the stream is the buzz of cicadas, sounding like an aggregation of irritated rattlesnakes. The sound builds to a crescendo on one side of the creek, then crosses to the other side. Then one section stops and the sound moves downstream like a train moving away into the distance. It stops completely and all of a sudden starts up again, seeming to burst out of the trees.

Sonoita Creek used to be much larger, but it's been reduced, according to Robin, "by diversion for irrigation, municipal use in town, effects of grazing in the water basin up where the water gathers. Up at Fort Buchanan . . . back in the 1800s when the soldiers came through the Sonoita area they had to go around the edge of the valley, and through the foothills of the mountains because it was too boggy to pass through, too swampy. They'd ride along Sonoita Creek on horseback and the grasses were overhead.

"There are still some guys in town who remember jumping on the train in town as kids and jumping off when it got to the creek, to fish and play in the creek all day, then jump on someone's burro and ride it back

Vermilion flycatcher. (N. Snyder)

into town."

The sanctuary was originally land grant property, first granted in 1823. It had several owners before it was purchased in 1966 by the Nature Conservancy. It is the oldest Nature Conservancy preserve in the state.

While we talk, a young boy and his mother walk up. Robin says, "Hi, Dave." The boy says hi and they sit down near us. "What are you doing out of school?"

"Oh, I got kicked out."

"Misbehaving," his mother says.

Robin talked to the boy and his mother for awhile and then returned to us. The boy was eating a banana and when he finished, he cocked his arm to throw the peel into the creek. Robin said, "Don't do that!"

"Why, the fish will eat it."

"No, they won't. Put it in the garbage can on your way out." The boy tossed the peel in the water.

His mother went down and picked it up and said, "I'll throw these where Robin won't see. The birds will eat it." Then she tossed the peels into the shrubs.

Robin asked her, "Why would the birds eat it?"

"Our chickens eat orange peels."

Without much further discussion, the pair wandered off, down a trail. After they left, Robin said, "Those people live in town. They don't stay on the trails, he'll throw his banana peels into the bushes. They used to walk up and down the creek, even though I asked them to stay on the trails a zillion

times, but I can't turn into the hard-ass on these guys because that's the kid who when he grows up will be breaking into the donation box, or stealing postcards, if he doesn't like this place. He's gotta like it.

"The local people are not environmentally conscious, this is just their backyard and playground. When his mom grew up, she probably came down here camping. His dad likes the place a lot, because the first full-time manager, when he was putting in trails, hired high school kids and his dad was one of the people who built the trails. He'll give it nominal respect, but it's largely because he knows me and I'm friends of the family. It's respect for me, more than an environmental respect for the place. I'm a local-yokel to these people. I don't try to talk Mr. Science to them. They say, 'Well, this guy's all right. I wonder what he does down there?'

"Public attitudes vary. Most people appreciate the fact that it didn't turn into a subdivision or a golf course, but also they're resentful of the fact that they can't have their Fourth of July, Mother's Day, and Easter picnics in here too. So you get a basic support. A lot of people think it's a waste because it's not getting 'used.'

"They're recognizing the economic value more now than when I started. Back then we only got less than four thousand visitors a year. Now it's over twenty thousand. When you start to get those numbers you

can't help but notice. The guy who runs the motel thinks we're wonderful. That place is packed with birders, April, May, and June. The guy at the store, the restaurant, the market, all are doing a booming business because of the tourists."

The job of managing the preserve is a difficult balancing act—trying to protect the natural qualities of the area while accommodating the thousands of visitors and gaining the support of the locals. "The town of Patagonia dumps their sewer plant effluent right into Sonoita Creek . . . which means we have to be involved with the town of Patagonia and its public works department. They're directly affecting the quality of the stream.

"As long as the plant is operating efficiently, there's no problem at all. The water comes out probably cleaner than the water people in town get out of their taps, but if there's a problem in the plant, there's a problem in the stream, and we are direct neighbors, our upper end bounds the town. So we have to deal with them directly. It is a community-involvement situation here, unlike most of the other preserves, none of which actually bound a town."

Robin realizes that management also means living with change. "We can't make it like it used to be. Nothing in the universe is static. We're all rolling for-ward in time, so why should we expect to see anything stay the same forever. It's not going to change in my lifetime. If I come back here as an old man, I still expect to see cottonwoods towering overhead, but if you send my great-great-great-grandson down here, he may see something different."

Since 1980, when he came on as manager, he has seen the arrival of the sycamore trees. "They started growing in 1985. They were found upstream and downstream before. Channelization—degradation—of the streambed is keeping the normal annual floods from getting out into the floodplain, and that elevated terrace that's being created is not suitable germination conditions for willows and cottonwoods. So we're seeing an evolution into an ash/walnut forest from a cottonwood/willow forest. Willows and cotton-woods need to land on saturated soil and have to get their roots in wet soil and stay wet. You don't see ger-mination taking place on the banks."

We asked him what the prime asset of Patagonia is. "It's gotta be the creek. Anywhere you've got flowing water in this part of the state, you've got a jewel."

Why should a place like Patagonia-Sonoita Creek Sanctuary be preserved? The answer is simply put by Robin: "Because we need it. As people, we need it."

This massive gnarled old cottonwood is probably the most photographed tree in southeastern Arizona. It grows along one of the trails in the Patagonia Sanctuary. (H. Parent)

85

AQUATIC ENVIRONMENTS

SAN PEDRO RIVER— Mike Link

"At one time, the friendliest comment I heard was 'What the hell are you doing here?' " is the way Erich Campbell explains the beginning of the Bureau of Land Management's San Pedro Riparian National Conservation Area, perhaps the most exciting project in the controversial BLM's history.

This is the river that Coronado followed in his search for the seven cities of gold. Marshes filled the valley from end to end, behind a series of beaver dams. There were rich woodlands, thick growth of river cane, otters, elk, deer, turkey, quail, and thousands of acres of prairie dog towns. In the fall, the wetlands were full of waterfowl and shorebirds. Large fish, some reputed to be three feet long, lived in the stream.

The river flows north from the copper mining district of Cananea, Mexico, and empties into the Gila River in Arizona. A succession of mountains and hills parallels the river as it moves from the border past the shadow of Mount Lemmon.

Human history began when glacial ice still cooled the Canadian border. It was a time when elephants and mammoths roamed this area, a time when the hunters used Clovis points on their spears. There were giant beavers, sabre-toothed tigers, native horses, dire wolves, and giant short-faced bears in North America until that time, and their populations were compressed into the southern region because of the continental ice sheets of the North.

Scientists believe that all of these animals disappeared in two thousand years! The cause is unknown, but Paul Martin of the University of Tucson holds with the most dramatic theory, one in which the prehistoric Indians obliterated these animals through overhunting. Others have dubbed this the "Pleistocene overkill." In a history of many mass extinctions, this was the first one in which only the large mammals were eliminated. The evidence that is cited is the Clovis point found in various archaeological digs, like the one on the Lehner Ranch along the San Pedro.

Ed Lehner refers to this as a "used elephant lot" or "Pachyderm Preserve." Ed is a garrulous man who feeds the javelinas and quail and greets every guest with enthusiasm. He is a born storyteller from North Dakota, who grew up in New York City and graduated from Colgate with a degree in economics and Cornell with an advanced degree in animal husbandry and ornithology.

His path led to France in World War II, to White Plains, New York, to Tucson, and then to his ranch. It is easy to be lulled by Ed's charm and wit, to underestimate his understanding of what he is sharing. Ed worked as an ecologist for Phelps Dodge for thirteen years, trying to find plants that would grow on the toxic tailings. That work and his natural curiosity about life around him have made him an expert on many aspects of the San Pedro. It is fortunate that he is.

After a rainstorm, erosion in a gully on his ranch exposed a toothplate from a mammoth. Ed found it, recognized it, and immediately reported it to the Arizona State Museum. The storm had exposed one hundred feet of bones, and a project was established to investigate the site. One more big rain would have washed it away.

The excavation unearthed numerous bones of mammoth, bison, tapir, and horse. There were two hearths (bonfire areas), butchering tools, and fifteen projectile points. In the scientific report, they speculate that this was a hunting site, that the big game came to the river to drink and were driven into the deeper water, killed, and then dragged to a sandbar, where they were butchered and eaten.

The projectile points, which appear at other excavations in the valley, represent a severe departure from the agriculture-based cultures of the area. Scientists tend to believe that it was not just a change in the societal norms, but that perhaps another group moved into the area. Martin believes that the Clovis hunters crossed the Bering land bridge and came down the

The cottonwood grove along the San Pedro River is a birder's dream in springtime before the leaves fully emerge. (D. Lazaroff)

Canelo Hills Sanctuary is a place of protection for rare plants and wildlife. (H. Parent)

ice-free corridor just east of the Canadian Rockies, to a "garden of Eden."

Ed points out that in his backyard there were twelve mammoths and a mastodon. "If you figure how many can survive after twelve thousand years, you can figure what the population here might have been." Most of those killed were young, more vulnerable and better eating. "They weren't stupid. You want to kill a mammoth, you better kill a little one."

Archaeologist C. Vance Haynes sees a role for climate in this scenario. He reasons that the melting ice caps resulted in a rise in the sea level, and that interior water levels were lowered all over. This caused the animals to concentrate, which would make them more vulnerable. Other scientists say that climate was the only reason, that the hunting was extraneous.

Ed adds his thought: "There is a black layer over the bones that corresponds with the extinction of the megamammals. Dr. Martin claims that man was responsible for extinction. I can't buy that. I might agree that they were the absolute last straw, but my feeling is that it was the climate.

"December 7, 1978, it was fourteen below zero. All the upper parts of the mesquite froze. Nine inches of snow insulated the lower growth. This far from the Ice Age, we can still get such an aberration. How much more often and more dramatic could it have been nearer the Ice Age?"

The excavation also showed that the old sandbar had been covered by a swamp, excavated by an arroyo, and filled again, and less than a hundred years ago the current arroyo began its excavations. The San Pedro Valley is a broad alluvial-filled basin, with a floodplain one mile in width at the Lehner Ranch. Less than a hundred years ago, this area was a series of grassy swales, springs, and seeps. There would have been cottonwood, walnut, ash, and oak stands, and the river channel would have been only two to three feet deep.

Now the same site is a semiarid grassland; the river has a minimum amount of flow; mesquite, black-brush, creosote, and cat's-claw are encroaching; and the hardwoods are confined to the stream channel.

Since the days of the Clovis point, the river has had a mixed history. Father Kino found two thousand "souls" and fourteen villages along the river. He also reported agriculture supported by small irrigation ditches. And he called the area "lush." Then, like the Clovis point hunters, another Indian culture moved in—the Apaches, a nomadic and aggressive culture from the north. They conducted raids in the San Pedro Valley and prevented its development.

After Mexican independence, the riparian lands were granted to wealthy cattlemen, but the Apaches raised a fuss; and for fifteen more years the land was not developed. The Gasden Purchase gave the land to

Botteri sparrow. (D. Collister)

the United States, once again there was a renewal of cattle interest, and for a third time the Apaches kept it out. The Apaches were the most effective environmental protection that the river has had.

Then Texas John Slaughter moved his herds in, and ranching was here to stay. He stopped the rustlers who stole cattle in the United States, sold the cattle in Mexico, then stole it in Mexico and sold it back in the United States.

In 1878, Tombstone took river-bottom trees for its mines; in 1879, the town of Charleston diverted water for mining and milling. The beaver were mostly trapped out, the trees were cut for the railroad and the towns, wells were dug, and cattle were moving in. Humans were making all the changes.

Then nature added another wrinkle—an earthquake. Tombstone had never had water, but after the earthquake, the mines were flooded. The basin and range country is underlain by a complex system of cracks and faults. It is the result of upheaval and collapse, and it forms the plumbing for the springs that feed the river. The earthquake rerouted some of that flow. By 1890, the boom days were over.

Agriculture in the Mormon settlement of Saint David took water, and an outbreak of malaria prompted the drainage of some swampland. They tapped the springs with wells and began a process of removing groundwater faster than it could be

replaced. In some areas, nature has no way of recharging Arizona's groundwater.

The biggest change came with grazing. In 1883, there were 68,000 cattle. Three years later there were 156,000, and suddenly there were prodigious floods and erosion, even with less rain than there had been in the past. From 1846 to 1904 four of the eleven species of native fish were eliminated from the San Pedro. In the next forty-five years, four more species were lost. Stream beds that had been two to three feet deep were now ten to twenty-five.

With all that, Erich Campbell can still say, "This is the best broadleaf riparian community left in Arizona, and the project will protect thirty miles of it." There are 275 species of birds, 80 mammal species, and 25 species of reptiles and amphibians that exist along the corridor. There are regular visits by green kingfishers, and there are half the nesting gray hawks in the United States. With protection, researchers expect to get the bird count up to 350. The river is a funnel for migration. Every species of U.S. hawk passes through here at some time.

The plans are to manage the land in a way that enhances the natural environment, to encourage human use only when it is compatible with the natural systems. The future sounds good. The problems are water use in a rapidly growing Sierra Vista and Mexican water use (which we cannot control). The mines of

Cananea could open a well that would shut off the entire river.

CANELO HILLS CIÉNAGA — Mike Link

Canelo Hills is off the regular path of tourist wandering. The roads twist and turn in grassy foothills, and end at an 1880 adobe homestead. The setting appears much as it might have to the early homesteader — natural grass fields spreading out before us, the land sloping gradually to a woody copse, and a sedge-filled marshland. It is peaceful and quiet, which may be two rare and endangered qualities, but the really rare characteristic is the marsh — the ciénaga.

Reading the history of southeastern Arizona gives me the impression that water wasn't always so restricted, although it has always been the primary influence in human settlement. The Pimas Altos had semipermanent villages near perennial water sources, and Father Kino and other early travelers noted that many of the washes had almost constant water flow and the "land was dotted with ciénagas." Today, ciénagas are in need of preservation and resurrection.

Our walk through the three distinct communities — grassland, riparian, and marshland — provided us with a nice dose of privacy. We met no other people all afternoon, and our official welcomer was a Say's phoebe in the barn. White-tailed deer enjoyed the trail too, and northern harriers swept across the grasslands with their long wings slightly raised, giving them a shallow V shape, as opposed to the flat line of other hawks. They cruise near the ground looking for reptiles and rodents.

Canelo Hills is home to the Montezuma quail and yellow-billed cuckoo. Botteri sparrows live in the grasses, and the Arizona form of the eastern bluebird nests in natural cavities.

This is one of the last of the natural ciénagas. It is home to the Canelo ladies' tresses, the only place in the state where they grow, and to other rarities, like the green rat snake, rock rattlesnake, black-tailed rattlesnake, and a variety of amphibians.

This is the headwaters of O'Donnell Creek, a permanent stream that can support the Gila chub, Gila sucker, and other fish that are endangered because of the scarcity of habitat. The chubs are large enough fish to have been a food source for the Indians, but management of fisheries in Arizona concentrated on introduced game fish rather than native animals.

Drainage, pollution, channelization, diversion, dams, and competition from introduced species has cost Arizona most of its native population of fish. But fish are nearly invisible to the casual observer. There are no fish listers that I know of, no one who travels with snorkel and mask to try and see all the native fish. They are hidden in an aquatic world, their demise is too easily missed, and they are too seldom defended.

The headwaters are fed by a spring and protected from headward erosion by a stabilization dam, a low structure that does not alter anything but the potential for destruction. The open-water area has three types of willow: Goodding, coyote, and swamp, which can leaf out with roots that are constantly in water. The shallow wetlands are filled with sedges, rushes, and a few grasses. Both areas trap nutrients from the deciduous growth on the slopes.

Aquatic insect life shares its home with the vertebrates, both those that live in the water and those that depend on the ciénaga for drinking. In addition, there is an evolutionary ancestor to the molluscs that inhabited the larger lakes of the tertiary (dinosaur) period — the tiny hydrobiid molluscs.

Refuge manager Robin Baxter observes, "Canelo Hills is a really good example of how the Nature Conservancy goes about their purchases. On less than three hundred acres there are three specific habitats to protect." All warrant protection individually. The refuge has an endangered fish, pygmy mice, rock rattlesnakes, and Mexican garter snakes, and the sanctuary harbors rare plants. "Rather than spread their energies around, the Nature Conservancy looks for the prize, the jewels . . . and I also like it because it is so peaceful and quiet."

During our short visit we encountered a rattlesnake that probably didn't enjoy us infringing on its territory, and we came away with a good feeling for the site. But the real bonus came when we sat on the porch steps to cool off. As we stared down the road, we caught movement in the grass, a bending of the blades that was out of sync with the ripples of the wind. Often when this happens, the cause never appears. This day, a bobcat stepped out, and moved quickly away from us and back into the grasses. Sometimes a glimpse is all that is needed to form a lifetime impression.

Black-tailed rattlesnake. (D. Lazaroff)

Bobcat. Sometimes a glimpse forms a lifetime image. (N. Snyder)

PERSPECTIVE

BY MIKE LINK

When my son Matt was still in junior high, he accompanied me and a class of college students to southeastern Arizona. It was a heady trip for a young boy—new sights, adventure, and a close-knit group of students who befriended him.

We visited many of the mountain ranges, saw hundreds of birds, romped in a midday monsoon, watched streams fill with flash floods, camped, visited with strangers, took showers on the military base, bought ice cream in the towns, let tarantulas walk over our hands, and called to owls at night.

Our class met John McIntyre, a 95-year-old pioneer who lived in the near-ghost town of Sunnyside. He said he was there to be an evangelist to travelers like us. The Sunnyside missionary wore a butcher's apron as his frock, because of a man he met in Nogales. He didn't know the man, but he liked the looks of the apron.

Matt remembers sitting in the shade of a walnut listening to John and his stories of life in a religious mining community. He also remembers driving down a clay road in the rain, with students on both sides of the van to keep it from sliding off the road, and me at the wheel keeping the tires moving.

Birds, coatis, people, places. It was our best trip together, and the memories grow more precious each year. Southeastern Arizona has become a personal part of our father-son love, and I love the area as a result.

But there are problems here, webs of wires reaching in all directions, oblivious to the scenic cost. Air pollution fills a valley once known for healthy, warm, dry air. From a plane, green clusters mark golf courses, and they stand out from the desert. Green means water, and Tucson has very little. The town advocates growth, yet ecology says all organisms need water. To grow without it is a suicidal folly.

This is a fragile landscape, a region of rare, endangered, and endemic creatures. We threaten it with our misuse, but we possess the knowledge to understand the land and to prosper with it. The national forest and monuments preserve much of the Catalina and Rincon mountains, but only part of the Tucson range. Now those ragged peaks are confronted with an onslaught of development that will change their face.

People come here for health, not to breathe polluted air. They come for open space, not crowding. They come to enjoy and observe the unusual treasures of nature, not to mourn their loss.

In the end the "sky islands" can be biological treasures, or tragedies. Their fate is in human hands.

ACKNOWLEDGMENTS

Our Arizona experiences have been enriched by the people we have met. We learned from them, we discovered through them, and the text reflects many of their ideas and insights which are now incorporated into our view of southeastern Arizona. The purpose of this acknowledgment is to say thanks and to let you, the reader, know that the book has benefited from the input of many people; the region has many stories to be told and levels to be understood.

There are many people to thank and to those we miss, we apologize.

Thanks to Robin Baxter, and Debbie and Tom Collazo of the Nature Conservancy; Wade Sherbrooke of the Southwest Research Station; Debbie Sanders—park ranger at Chiricahua National Monument; and Bill Hoy, historian and former manager at Fort Bowie.

Carol Moore and the staff of Lazy K Bar Ranch; Bob and Leslie Cote, Jerry Brewer, Chuck Corchran, and Joe the wrangler at Tanque Verde Ranch; and Eve and Gerry Searle of Grapevine Ranch. We had wonderful adventures at each place.

Dave and Lyle Collister in Madera Canyon; Carol Cochran at the Arizona Sonora Desert Museum; Erich Campbell of the San Pedro River Project; Ed Lehner and his used elephant lot; Noel and Helen Snyder and the parrots; Ed Pilley and the national parks.

Then there was Miss Lillie Harrington and Elizabeth Husband; Win Bundy; James Babcock; John McIntyre; Vern Dormann. All these people added depth to this complex picture.

ORGANIZATIONS

We expect that after reading the text you will want more information about particular areas or locations. The following directory is designed to help you make contacts and learn more about southeastern Arizona.

American Museum of Natural History
Southwestern Research Station
Portal, AZ 85632

Amerind Foundation, Inc.
P.O. Box 248
Dragoon, AZ 85609

Arizona Nature Conservancy
300 East University Boulevard, Suite 230
Tucson, AZ 85705

Arizona State Parks
800 West Washington, Suite 415
Phoenix, AZ 85007

Arizona-Sonora Desert Museum
2021 West Kinney Road
Tucson, AZ 85743

Arizona Office of Tourism
1100 West Washington
Phoenix, AZ 85007

Audubon Society—Tucson
300 East University Boulevard, Suite 120
Tucson, AZ 85705

Catalina State Park
P.O. Box 36986
Tucson, AZ 85740

Chiricahua National Monument
Dos Cabezas Route, Box 6500
Willcox, AZ 85643

Cochise Hotel
P.O. Box 27
Cochise, AZ 85606

Coronado National Forest
300 West Congress Street
Tucson, AZ 85701

Coronado National Monument
R.R. 1, Box 126
Hereford, AZ 85615

Fort Bowie National Historic Site
P.O. Box 158
Bowie, AZ 85605

Friends of Madera Canyon
P.O. Box 1203
Green Valley, AZ 85622

Grapevine Canyon Ranch, Inc.
P.O. Box 302
Pearce, AZ 85625

Lazy K Bar Ranch
8401 North Scenic Drive
Tucson, AZ 85743

Mile Hi/Ramsey Canyon Preserve
R.R. 1, Box 84
Hereford, AZ 85615

Patagonia-Sonoita Creek Sanctuary
P.O. Box 815
Patagonia, AZ 85624

Sabino Canyon Visitors Center
5700 North Sabino Canyon Road
Tucson, AZ 85715

Saguaro National Monument
3693 South Old Spanish Trail
Tucson, AZ 85730

San Xavier del Bac Mission
Route 11, Box 645
Tucson, AZ 85746

Singing Wind Bookstore
Benson, AZ 85602

Southwest Parks and Monuments Association
221 North Court
Tucson, AZ 85701

Tanque Verde Ranch
Route 8, Box 66
Tucson, AZ 85748

Tumacacori Mission National Monument
P.O. Box 67
Tumacacori, AZ 85640

ABOUT THE AUTHORS

Mike Link traveled to southeastern Arizona for over a decade before writing this book. He has used the mountains and deserts in teaching college students ecology, leading birding expeditions, and exploring for personal pleasure.

As director of Northwoods Audubon Center, Mike also is an instructor for Northland College and the University of Minnesota at Duluth. His published works include *Journeys to Door County, The Black Hills/Badlands, Outdoor Education, Grazing,* and a series of biographical books about the conservationist Sigurd Olson. His two children grew up sharing outdoor experiences with him; now Matthew is an outdoor education major and Julie enjoys the outdoors on horseback.

Kate Crowley has explored southeastern Arizona in every season. Born and raised in Minnesota, she has found the desert and "sky islands" of Arizona to be a dramatic and exciting contrast in environments.

Kate's skills as a naturalist and writer were developed during her nine years at the Minnesota Zoo, where she supervised the monorail interpretive program and wrote articles for zoo publications. Her knowledge of wildlife and wilderness grew with participation in volunteer bird censusing for the Minnesota River Valley Wildlife Refuge and involvement with local conservation and environmental groups, as well as extensive travel in the United States and abroad. Kate is the proud mother of Alyssa and Jonathon, who live in Willow River, Minnesota, with her and Mike.

Mike and Kate were married aboard the ketch *Izmir* and sailed Lake Superior on their honeymoon. They are coauthors for the Voyageur Press wildlife and wild lands series, including *Love of Loons, Boundary Waters Canoe Area Wilderness, Lake Superior's North Shore and Isle Royale,* and *Apostle Islands National Lakeshore.*

The gila monster is a venomous, but shy and retiring, lizard. (G. Huey)